WARTE MAL!
PROSTITUTION AFTER
THE VELVET REVOLUTION
ANN-SOFI SIDÉN

Hayward Gallery

Published on the occasion of the exhibition *Warte Mal!: Prostitution After the Velvet Revolution*, organized by the Hayward Gallery, London, 17 January – 1 April 2002

Exhibition organized by Clare Carolin, assisted by Sophie Allen

Catalogue designed by SMITH
Printed in England by P.J. Print
Front cover: Legs, Motel Hubert, 2001. C-print
Frontispiece: Prostitute in window, Cheb, 1999. C-print
Published by Hayward Gallery Publishing, London SE1 8XX, UK
© Hayward Gallery 2002
Diaries, interviews and images © Ann-Sofi Sidén 2002
Essay by Robert Fleck © Robert Fleck 2002

ISBN 1 85332 225 3

Hayward Gallery Publishing titles are distributed outside North and South America and Canada by Cornerhouse Publications, 70 Oxford Street, Manchester M1 5NH (tel. 0161 200 1503; fax. 0161 200 1504).

CONTENTS

It is a pleasure and an honour to present at the Hayward Gallery the first British showing of Ann-Sofi Sidén's video installation *Warte Mal!*. Born in Stockholm in 1962, over the past ten years Sidén has emerged on the international scene as one of the more notable figures of her generation. Her work has been shown at the Biennale of São Paulo and at *Manifesta 2* in 1998, at the Carnegie International and the Venice Biennale in 1999, at the South London Gallery in 2000, and at the Musée d'art Moderne de la Ville de Paris in 2001. In 2001, her film *QM, I think I call her QM*, 1997 was included in the Hayward's programme of National Touring Exhibitions as part of *Trauma*, which was shown at Dundee Contemporary Arts, Firstsite, Colchester and the Museum of Modern Art, Oxford.

Sidén's practice shifts confidently between the mediums of film, video, installation, sculpture and performance and is informed by an understanding of process-based and conceptual art of the 1960s and 1970s, much of which was produced in response to political tensions of the time. Now, as the exponential production of images, the mechanics of the mass media and a culture of surveillance remove us ever further from the human realities of global politics, Sidén's skill as an artist is to re-deploy the devices of image-making in order to expose, rather than conceal, the truth. *Warte Mal!* is at once a compelling work of art and a comprehensive social document. It succeeds on both counts by addressing the economic, political and historical forces behind the collapse of Communism through personal and individual circumstances and by doing so with acute wisdom and compassion.

We would like above all to thank Ann-Sofi Sidén for making this showing of *Warte Mal!* possible, for collaborating with us on its presentation and installation and for her involvement in the production of this book. Her commitment, energy and attention to detail have carried this project forward and working with her has been both stimulating and a great pleasure.

We are grateful to Robert Fleck for the essay which appears here and the knowledge and insight which it brings to bear both on *Warte Mal!* and on Sidén's practice. I also thank Adam Hooper of SMITH for his considered approach to the design of this book, and Linda Schofield, the Hayward's Art Publisher, for her meticulous attention to its editing and production needs . My thanks also go to Caroline Wetherilt, the Hayward's Publishing Co-ordinator, and Clare Hennessy for their assistance, particularly with the interview transcriptions.

We are grateful as well to Sofia Bertilsson at Galerie Nordenhake in Berlin who gave us invaluable advice in all matters relating to the not inconsiderable production needs of the work, and to Martine Pasquet and Julia Garimorth at the Musée d'art Moderne de la Ville de Paris, particularly during the early stages of the project.

Tom Cullen has been responsible for overseeing the complexities of resolving the audio-visual requirements of *Warte Mal!*, and we thank him for his expertise and attentiveness. Thanks must also go to David Dernie for reconfiguring the design of the installation to complement the spaces of the Hayward Gallery, and to Lightwaves Ltd for their assistance with the exhibition's lighting requirements.

Felicity Allen, the Hayward's Head of Public Programmes, and Cathy Haynes, our Public Programmes Co-ordinator, have worked closely with Ann-Sofi Sidén to devise an extensive series of talks, events and seminars to complement the exhibition. I am grateful to them and to all those at the Hayward Gallery who have worked so hard to make this exhibition a success: Ann Berni and Arwen Fitch in Hayward Press; Avril Scott, the Hayward's Head of Marketing; Keith Hardy, the Hayward's Head of Operations and Mark King, the Hayward's Installation Manager. Fiona Bradley, one of the Hayward Exhibitions Curators, has championed the project throughout, and Martin Caiger-Smith, Head of Exhibitions, has overseen its delivery. Very special thanks go to Sophie Allen, Assistant Exhibition Organiser on the project, for her skill, efficiency and tireless attention to all matters relating to the installation of the show, and to Clare Carolin, the Hayward's Exhibitions Curator responsible for bringing this provocative and timely undertaking to fruition.

Susan Ferleger Brades Director, Hayward Gallery

Ann-Sofi Sidén's Diary

Motel Hubert, Dubi, the Czech Republic 02/99 – 10/99

06/02/99   10:00 p.m. I am sitting in the bar of the Motel Hubert. My translator and I sleep in rooms upstairs. This is not a regular motel.

A working class German man in a jean jacket enters the bar. He goes up to Katja and kisses her on the hand.

Katja is the bartender here. She and her husband Honza own the motel. They seem like a modern couple but Katja seems to be doing all the hard work, every night.

Honza has a son, Honza Jr., from a previous marriage. Honza Jr. is a typical want-to-be young playboy. When he has to work, he passes the time by flirting and teasing the girls.

The German has ordered a beer and sits down. Liba sits next to him. She speaks only a little German.

Liba is owned by the gypsies, Vlado and Vlasta. Liba takes off her jacket. Her small breasts almost fall out. He stares at her breasts as she leans over and points at the large hole in his T-shirt. He is so fat his chest and half his stomach are exposed. This man is really drunk. He mutters something she seems to understand. He walks up to the bar and pays for her.

She picks up her bag and goes over to the window where Andrea sits alone. Andrea doesn't have a pimp. She is her own boss. She pays Honza and Katja 20 per cent of her earnings to work out of the motel.

Liba whispers something to her. The German, key in hand, escorts Liba behind the bar through the kitchen and up to a room.

11:15 p.m. Vanja! Vanja is here now. Another one of her steady clients just arrived. Vanja's clients are very different to Liba's. Like Andrea, Vanja also works on her own. She has a Bulgarian boyfriend. When she talks about him, it sounds like he is her pimp as well. Her client tonight is a small Italian man with a mustache. He offers Vanja a rose. Katja shows off a bouquet of roses.

Vanja screams, 'Oh, she gets a whole bouquet and I just get one rose!'.

The Italian client says, 'But you are smaller.'

'No, no, Katja is smaller', Vanja says.

He hands Vanja a small white plastic bag. Another present. She opens it right away. It's an Armani watch. Vanja's happy now. He kisses her on the cheek.

Liba is back in the window looking jealously at both of them. Vanja's cellphone rings. She gets up and leaves the Italian client.

07/02/99 10:30 a.m. Sleeping here is not like sleeping anywhere else. I just woke up. There is a lot of snow outside. Last night, I heard the girls howling, 'warte mal ... warte mal!', over and over into the morning. And sometimes I hear dogs barking. Vanja complains that she's often woken up by the rooster in the backyard around 7 a.m.. That means she has slept only two hours. A girl, finding herself alone in a remote extended 'red-light district' in the Czech mountains.

08/02/99 2:00 p.m. In 1938, this area along the Czech border was occupied by Hitler. The Czechs were forced out of their homes and moved to the centre of the country. They left behind all of their possessions. German families were moved in. A year later, 15 March 1939, Hitler claimed all of Czechoslovakia. After the war, new borders were drawn. The Germans were sent home to their country. The Czech people slowly moved back to these border towns. Many houses remained empty and deteriorated. Factories, run by Germans during the war, were abandoned. Today, Germans return to visit the graveyards. Some Czechs fear the Germans may one day come back and attempt to reclaim their property.

11:30 p.m. This evening we continue our interview with Vanja. Towards the end her cellphone rings. Twice, we are interrupted. She has a German client waiting downstairs. He looks like a cultivated businessman, or a professor of economics, or a dentist or something. Good-looking, in his late thirties. He holds her hand. It's cute to see them together like this, like a couple. His coat is still on. The car is running outside. He touches her arm gently. He is a real gentleman. Vanja's dressed in white short-shorts and a tiny yellow top. Most of her slim body is bare. She has on her high platforms with the leopard skin pattern. Together they go outside into the snow. They talk in the freezing cold. They agree on something and she comes back in rubbing her arms. I think he came in with no money and is going to a bank machine.

Videostills, 1999. *Girls in and around Dubi, winter*

Vanja disappears upstairs for a while. She comes back wearing long black pants and the yellow top. It's interesting to compare Vanja's clients. On Friday she met with that small Italian man with curly hair, long in the back, with pilot glasses who hardly speaks any German.

10/02/99   9:00 p.m. Vanja's playing Bulgarian pop music: '... If God had a cellphone we could make some black market business ... If God had a cellphone I could have a red Ferrari and he could have a Ferrari too ...'.
Vanja is putting on her make-up. She's a bit withdrawn. Radek and I order vodka drinks. The atmosphere changes. Vanja starts talking to us, Radek translates.
She tells us Katja is her best friend. She brags how this past Christmas Katja gave her a ring. All the other girls got soap and shampoo. Vanja says if she left, Katja would have no one to talk to: 'Once, I got really drunk and insulted Katja's husband, Honza. I called him a paedophile. A greedy, horny old man who tries to save money by turning down the heat in the motel. He got really mad at me. He told me to leave. The next morning I was packing my bags when Honza came in and asked what I was doing. I told him I was leaving, like he said! "No, don't leave." And he left my room.
If I left, Katja would have no one to talk to.'

12/02/99   3:00 p.m. The Motel Hubert has a guard dog, Danni. He is inside the bar now. He's a young dog, only eight months old. Danni used to belong to Vlado the gypsy pimp. The two were playing in the street when a car hit Danni. He would have died if Katja hadn't saved him. Now she complains that the dog gets too much food from the cook, Kveta. The dog jumps all over Katja. Vanja calls for Danni but he doesn't listen to her. Her attention moves to Vlado.
'Are you scared of Danni?', she asks. The tiny gypsy man says, 'yes, yes'. Vanja tells me, 'I asked if he's been bitten. "Yes, yes!".' She imitates him and laughs.
Vlado and his wife, Vlasta, are both very short. They own the young, insecure girl, Liba. They push her to be more aggressive with the clients.

Liba always looks very sad and shy. Sometimes she sings along with the pop music.

13/02/99   6:15 p.m. Today I met with the police chief here in Dubi. He believes that the gypsies will make themselves extinct through drugs like heroin. He says no one buys drugs from them because they cut it with plaster and salt so they end up selling it to their own people. He compares their situation to that of the American Indians.
Of course he said all of this off camera as we were leaving.

15/02/99   4:05 p.m. The police chief said to me, 'I don't like Lenin but he was right when he said what is most important in life is to learn, learn and learn.'
Talking about criminals, he said, 'A donkey is dangerous in the front. A horse is dangerous from behind. And an idiot is dangerous all around.'
He also told me that his wife wants to become a painter. For his interview, he wanted to be seated in front of a romantic painting depicting a woman and a child, he claimed it was made by a famous Czech artist.

14/04/99   8:00 p.m. I am back again. The gypsy pimps Vlado, Vlasta, Martino and Maruska are hanging out in the Motel Hubert bar while their girls, Liba and Marcela, work.
The pimps are watching some film on TV. The film's in Czech. It seems to be a satire about World War II. I can tell they're engaged in the film by their laughter and comments.
Marcela comes in to get a cigarette from the table. They ask her not to stand in the way of the TV. Marcela doesn't move. Very calmly, she lights her cigarette and says they have to wait.

10:05 p.m. Two gypsy women walk in with their goods in plastic bags. They are going from bar to bar tonight selling their merchandise. This is how the girls shop for clothes, shoes, make-up and accessories.
Andrea is shown piece after piece. A white shirt with blue polka dots, a lady's suit, a body suit, a g-string, a turquoise bikini and a red top. Now the ponytail wigs: blond and brunette, curly or

straight. Andrea is interested in the long, curly one. She asks how much it costs. It's 100 Korunas.

'Saturday, come back on Saturday when I have money', she says. The gypsies leave and two Czech men walk in. They want to rent the Red Bar next door to Motel Hubert. It has been vacant since Petko fled and was later arrested. Honza sits down to talk business with them. They want to start Friday with three or four Russian girls.

Katja says there will be a big soccer game in Teplice on Tuesday. The match will be between a Czech team (Teplice) and a Dortmund team (Borussia) from Germany. This means a lot of men will pass through Dubi on their way to the match and on their way back to Germany.

25/07/99 Today at the lake I see the local people's reactions to us.

Eva is with us today. I met her through Petra, who used to work at Motel Hubert. Now both of them work at the Falk Bar. Eva comes up to me while I am standing in line to buy some drinks. She stands out because of her comical appearance. Her long lanky legs. Her missing teeth. Her whimsical gestures.

A couple in their thirties look at us and point to where Radek and Katja are sitting. I would pay a thousand Korunas to know what they are saying.

Everybody knows everybody here. Katja says she sometimes runs into women whose husbands have been to the Motel Hubert, fucking the girls.

Eva doesn't change into a swimsuit. She can't relax for a minute on the blanket. Instead, she shows me photos of her ex-boyfriends. All the shots were taken at the military barracks. Young men with shaved heads doing pranks or lined up as best buddies in the dorms or cafeterias.

Eva also keeps notebooks, the pages are cluttered with drawings of logos for Nike, Adidas, Coca-Cola – all her favourite brands. Some of the pages are tedious transcriptions from a book about the marijuana plant. She also lets her friends write in it.

29/07/99 Eva tells me she is in love with my translator, Radek. Everybody already knows. She says that she can't sleep or think about anything but Radek.

Videostills, 1999. (top row) *Relatives' photos of missing girls posted in the Dubi Police Station* (bottom left) *Ann-Sofi Sidén, her translator and a policeman at the Dubi Police Station* (bottom right) *Chief of Police in Dubi*

'Sofi you must help me!'
She flirts with him by crawling around on all fours, popping up
from behind the bar or outside the window like a jack-in-the-box.
'I don't want to fight, just talk to him. But Petra is also in love
with him.'
Radek and I ran into Eva at the gas station. We walked her up to
the Falk Bar. Her aggressive playfulness reveals her love. When
she confessed her love to me she said, 'I never really liked men
with long hair.'

30/07/99   Vlado announces to the bar that it's Liba's birthday tomorrow.
Honza Jr. says laughing, 'I have a birthday present for you.'
'What?', Liba asks.
'A nice gift for you, Vlado will pay me to screw you up in the
room.' Vlado, the gypsies and everybody at the table laughs their
heads off.
Liba is always the butt of the joke.

31/07/99   5:45 p.m. Andrea is at the bar with one of her regular clients. He
is a German guy, big and fat and red from the sun. They are both
wearing track suits. Andrea isn't wearing any make-up today.
They make a funny, ironic couple in their sport suits. He is so fat
and out of shape. He walks away for a moment. She whispers to
me, 'I don't want to have sex with him today. I told him I have my
period but I don't.' He returns with a CD player and headphones.
He puts the headphones on her head. She listens and makes
faces to us.
A small gypsy boy walks in with a horribly burnt and twisted
face. Andrea's client gives him 50 Korunas. She says the gypsy
boy's father is probably sitting in a bar up the street spending all
the money the boy brings in on drinks and slot machines. There
are a lot of these gambling halls here, close to the German border.

6:42 p.m. Andrea and the German man are still hanging out
together here in the bar. He is paying for her time.
A Czech guy comes in selling a set of six glasses and a meat-
slicer, still packaged. The German client buys the glasses
for Andrea.
Vlado and Martino drop off Marcela and Liba for work. Marcela's

pimp, Martino, used to be a champion boxer. He gives Liba a rose still wrapped in plastic foil. I bought her a soft pink bunny purse to wear around her waist. I don't know if the other girls gave her anything.

She looks happier today. It's her twenty-first birthday.

7:30 p.m. Michal stopped by the Motel Hubert earlier in the afternoon. He is Eva and Petra's pimp. They refer to him as boss. All the same, he takes 50 per cent. He drives a red sports car. This is the first time I've actually seen him. He's a massive, muscular guy. Younger than I expected, maybe twenty-five. Michal shows Katja a fresh tattoo on his right biceps, still oily. After he left, Katja told me that once he and his bodyguards came into Motel Hubert and shot a Bulgarian guy in the arm. There was blood all over the walls. Katja cleaned up and did not call the police. The next day, Michal came in and apologized to her. Now he's moving the girls down to the Red Bar adjacent to the Motel Hubert. His bar, the Falk Bar, was sold to some gypsies.

01/08/99   I went to bed at six o'clock this morning. We partied all night at the Falk Bar. By 5 a.m. we were back here at the Motel Hubert. We ordered more drinks, Andrea played her favourite music by FARKAN.

A blond Russian woman sat alone at the end of our table. She ordered drinks and food, waving a 100 Deutschmark bill. No one knew her. She was drunk when we arrived. Katja spoke to her in Russian. Eva and I were filming in the bar. Marcela told us we should not point the camera at this woman. She hardly touched her food.

Katja wanted to close the restaurant so she asked the woman to leave. Radek, Eva and Katja helped her out into a bright morning. She could hardly walk. They asked her where she was going. She didn't know. She said she had escaped from her pimp and had stolen 3000 Deutschmarks from him.

She was dressed in a beige outfit that made her look like an Eastern European office worker. She had a handbag and a plastic bag with her. We wanted to put her in a cab, help her get out of there. She was too drunk to want anything.

Then her Russian pimp showed up. She cried as he put her in his

Videostills, 1999. (top left) *Natasha and a customer, Motel Hubert* (top right) *Andrea and Marcela, Motel Hubert* (bottom left) *Eva and Radek at the Falk Bar* (bottom right) *Vanja and a tarot reader, Motel Hubert*

car. Radek argued with him. Her pimp got really nasty. 'What do you want? Yeah, and what do you want?', he kept threatening. Radek backed off. The Russian pimp drove off with the woman.

This afternoon, Eva went to the bar where the Russian woman works. The girls there told her that she had been beaten up really badly.

3:45 p.m. Katja says Eva is worried about the interview. She wonders what I'm going to ask.

Eva is very emotional. She started crying when she heard the Whitney Houston song, 'I Will Always Love You'.

02/08/99   11:00 a.m. Katja told Radek that she and Honza had a really bad argument that morning. Honza's mood can turn ugly from drinking, and this was one of those periods.

In his fit of paranoia and anger, Honza fired Katja, his own wife! And then fired his son, Honza Jr.. He thinks they are conspiring against him. He has lost his mind a little. Katja is such a small, delicate woman.

Before Katja left for the day she warned Marcela that Honza was drunk. She said he might return and be nasty to the girls.

The gypsy pimps heard this and got really mad. 'We don't need to take this bullshit from the Czechs!', they said.

05/08/99   Last night, Radek drove Katja to a bar late at night to pick up the car from Honza, who was too drunk to drive. It was Honza who had suggested to Katja on the phone that Radek should drive her down. When they arrived Honza asked her jealously why she didn't just leave with Radek.

Today, Honza showed up at the bar and asked Radek to help him prepare the grill out in the backyard. Honza looked hungover and emotionally drained – a fallen ex-communist waiter.

I came down from my room at noon. Kveta, the cook, had made some potatoes. Honza asked if I wanted to use the grill in the backyard. Kveta offered me some of the potatoes she had prepared that morning.

Honza said, 'No, I don't think she would like your potatoes! I don't like them!'. He was really nasty to everybody around him.

3:00 p.m. The girls are really upset over Radek. Petra told Andrea
that Radek slept with her. It's not true. But Andrea's jealous and
thinks Radek should now sleep with her as well.
'Come on, let's go up to the room and fuck! You can have some of
my pussy!', Andrea says.
They argue over him constantly, but in a playful way, competing
to see which of them is going to be the one who gets 'the
translator' into bed and prove he is just another man.
But for Eva it seems more serious.

6:00 p.m. I shot some photos of Marcela, Andrea and Liba.
Andrea said, 'I'm totally out of it today!'. They don't want to
be here.
Marcela has worked as a prostitute for three and a half years.
Before that she worked for some electric company. She's tired
today because she only slept for fifty minutes. These girls work
twelve hours or more seven days a week. Every now and then
they get one day off.
Marcela has very articulate body language. When standing out
on the street she'll grab her crotch indicating she has good
pussy. Or pat her crotch like it's a cute little animal, point at
some guy walking by or give passing cars the finger.

06/08/99   5:40 p.m. Radek and I drove Eva to the Falk Bar. I sat in the
backseat. She attacked him with the pen I bought her while we
were shopping in Teplice that afternoon. She drew little blue
marks all over his legs, arms and face. He was covered in blue
ink. He tried politely to make her stop but he could hardly drive
the car with her there.
She attacks him whenever she has a chance. She'll attack him
with sand, dry flowers, anything!
Last night she called him twice, waking him up at 4 and 5 a.m..
I tried explaining to her that he has a girlfriend but it doesn't
matter to her.

11:30 p.m. Andrea says she had a client without any teeth. She
says he smelt bad and had dirty hair.
'This client should go with Liba', she says, 'they suit each other'.
Liba allows herself to be intimidated again and again. Andrea

Videostills, 1999. *Girls along the road between Cheb and Dubi, summer*

then announces she has to go to the toilet: 'Will make some
chocolate for you Liba ...'.
I am surprised Andrea makes these jokes at Liba. I never saw her
as that type of girl. Everyone laughs their heads off.
I ask Liba how she lost her front teeth. Marcela says she had
a bad pimp who hit her. Liba says it happened to her three
years ago.
Marcela is standing on the street waving to passing cars. She
checks out the licence plates. This is how she rates potential
clients. This game passes hours of time. Vlado stops by outside
in a new blue car. He opens the trunk and hands Marcela a crate
of beer. She brings it in.
Liba is sitting on a chair outside. Marcela sits on her lap. Then
Andrea sits on top of Marcela. Three girls on a chair! It looks funny.
I want to take a photo of them like that but Marcela says I can't.
Inside the gypsy pimps are eating at their table. Marcela walks
over and snatches some food from their plates: 'I say to the men,
can I try your eggs? They say I'm coming! The man has a sausage
and two eggs.'
Liba's pimp, Vlado, comes out with a sandwich for Liba. Andrea
takes a straw and extends her cigarette. She is inhaling the
smoke through the straw.

07/08/99   1:24 a.m. Eva stops by the Motel Hubert with freshly-painted,
red polka dotted nails. On her way out she starts talking to one
of three guys sitting at the bar having a beer. Katja asks her
to leave.
Eva knows she shouldn't take the Hubert girls' clients. Apparently
she's seen this guy as a client at the Falk Bar.

2:50 a.m. Two guys walk in. They look like intellectuals. They sit
down at a table. The three girls are all over them. One guy
chooses Andrea. Marcela and Liba walk back to the doorstep.
The second guy claims he wants to drink a beer and decide on a
girl later.
Five minutes later Marcela marches in with a huge dark man
with hair to his shoulders. He pays Katja and they go straight to
a room.
Liba is left out on the street.

3:00 a.m. A man comes in, his head is freshly shaven. He looks like an auto-mechanic. He says he's been drinking in a bar since 5 p.m.. A heavy drinker, he had made a bet with the bar owner. For a hundred beers he would shave his head.

He tells a story about how once he was so drunk he almost died: 'I looked death in her eyes.'

Katja asks, 'So, what did she look like?', and laughs.

He replies, 'you think I'm joking but ...'.

This man carries his money in his socks. He is a real entrepreneur. He's a clown. The guy has on large loose shorts. He pulls them in a suggestive way and says, 'I can't dance now because I have a hard-on.' Everybody just cracks up!

4:45 a.m. Five guys have come in. There are only three girls here. The sky is a beautiful pink, blue. The morning is coming.

Eva looks tired and lost. Petra's laughing. Andrea is always a professional.

When I leave, the guys wave for me to come and join them at their table! It's not the first time since I got here that I've attracted these types of looks. And not only from the clients. I've often felt the gypsies sizing me up: 'Oh, she can dance, she's not too fat ...'.

Today, I said jokingly in Italian, 'I love you', to Martino, the ex-boxer pimp. Marcela translated what I said. His reaction to my joke was to go get his wife. He came out with her under his arm. It was as if he were making a point to me that he has a real woman. He said to me, 'This is good quality.'

08/08/99   Marcela calls me to come outside. Down the road a woman is walking towards us. She is a very fat woman with dark hair. Marcela says, 'That one likes to talk. She talks too much.'

As the woman passes us she says to Marcela, 'Hi Michelka.' She adds a few words and passes us, continuing to move her heavy body up the hill along the street. Marcela says, 'She's not drunk enough ... you know she weighs 300 pounds. Her husband, only 150 pounds. He is skinny as a board. I asked him once how they made love. He said it's hard to find the way in under the folds in her belly.'

Fifteen minutes later the fat woman's husband passes by. He is a very skinny man wearing a jacket and a hat. He walks out into the middle of the street to avoid us on the sidewalk. Marcela screams, 'Hi!'. He returns her greeting lifting his hand to his hat, 'Sieg Heil!' ['Hail Victory!']. Marcela says, 'Er ist ganz Verruckt!' ['He's really crazy!'].

I was taken by surprise today hanging out with the girls on the stoop. Marcela opened up to me for the first time. I like Marcela very much. She told me she learned all her German working on the street, talking to Katja and to her customers.
She seems so communicative tonight. She starts by talking about how the girls flash the cars just to have some fun. 'Oh, why not? Since it's so boring to hang around waiting and waiting for cars and clients.' Katja calls Marcela 'the sex machine'. She has three to four clients a day or more.

Radek, Honza and I returned from our fishing trip empty handed. The girls saw our car and flashed their bare breasts, lifted up their skirts, and bent over laughing.
Honza said, 'They're crazy!'.
Quite often the girls would scream to the cars in unison, 'warte mal!'. Liba screamed it very aggressively. Once in a while a car would stop. Often they would drive up into the parking lot across the street from Motel Hubert, outside the Imbiss. The girls would then rush across the busy street, competing with the girls working from the Imbiss. They were like flies on a piece of meat: six to seven girls giving the client in the car their prices.
The three girls from Motel Hubert came back across the street together empty handed. Marcela said the girls over there charge only 40 Deutschmarks. They have dirty rooms. The gypsies charge even less, 25 Deutschmarks.
'See that girl down there?', Marcela said. 'In the red blouse and pants? She's twenty-seven years old. She does it without rubbers. She sucks dick without a rubber. You know, she does it vaginal. Then the clients want to do it anal with her. And then oral and ejaculate into her mouth. Everything, without a rubber. She does it all without a rubber.'
She went on in her broken German, 'I was in Strasbourg, it was better there. Lots of money but the Turks robbed the girls. We

Videostills, 1999. *Views along the roads between Prague, Cheb and Dubi*

had to bring the money to the pimp before we took the next client. I worked there for a month. I left the day before the big police raid. Yeah, you see, one of my clients was a policeman, he warned me. He got it for free. You see, some girl got syphilis and ended up in a hospital. The police went and talked to her, inquiring about her pimp.

She told them everything. Then they went around asking all the girls. You know the girls, they are so are stupid. They put their pimps in prison for five years. Would you do that? I wouldn't do that, it's stupid. The man had a family and kids. The girls have no money if he goes to prison.'

Marcela told me all this very quickly. The words were pouring out of her mouth. Occasionally, she looked to see if Maruska or Martino were watching her. And of course they were. Maruska came out. She told her to stop talking and work. Marcela stopped immediately. She turned to the two other girls who had been listening to her talk to me. They hadn't understood.

After that, Marcela hasn't said a word to me, which has made me really depressed. I feel the complete control and oppression the gypsy pimps have over the girls.

I went to bed and slept until 11:00. I got up, met Katja in the kitchen. She made me some food. I sat down and I watched the girls work the German clients. It's unfortunate that I will never get an interview with Marcela because her pimps will never allow it.

10:30 p.m. Katja told me that about six months ago, when business was really slow, like in February or so, Marcela was beaten badly by her pimp, Martino.

Marcela said she was in Strasbourg in March of this year. Now I realize she was probably forced to be there by her pimp, to make more money. It all makes sense in the absolutely absurd way that everything does around here.

09/08/99   5:00 p.m. A West German client thought I was a Czech prostitute. He started talking to me. He said he understood only a little Czech. He poured his heart out to me. His mother was from Croatia. He went on about his two years in the war. He fought in 1992 against the Serbs.

'I educated and disciplined the soldiers,' he said. 'The soldiers
came from Holland, Belgium, Switzerland … and so on. They
were all criminals and murderers. But they were OK boys. I had
sixty-five men, two of whom died in battle. It was their own fault.
They were stupid, those two. War is fucked up. And myself, I only
fought two times.'

'And how much did you earn?', I asked.

'800 Deutschmarks, the soldiers 600 Deutschmarks a month.
But war is shit! I don't do it anymore. Now, I sell Mercedes cars.
I had four years education in the military in Germany before I
went to Croatia.'

Then Honza came in and started telling stories about his diving
experiences. How he drove to the Red Sea and some other place
outside Jordan where he went down 30 metres and excavated an
old British hangar ship 100 metres long:

'It still carries all it's treasures, tanks, machine guns, and Harley
Davidson motorbikes. You could look but not touch. But I sat on
the motorbikes and everything was videotaped there under water.'
Honza's not a bad guy if he's sober. He said he would take
everyone to see the videotape later in the week. The tank ship
had been bombed by the Germans during the Second World War.

09/08/99   11:30 p.m. I sat down to talk to Katja. Marcela, who seems to
catch men like rain, came down with a client. Katja said something to in her Czech. I asked what she said.

'Before they went to the room, the young, neat-looking guy in
the shirt and shorts asked her if he could have anal sex with her.'
This is what Marcela told Katja when the guy paid Katja for the
room.

And when Marcela came down she said, 'Katja! I got out of it.'
Katja was quick to point out that Marcela is a professional and
knows what to say. 'Besides,' she said, 'it was too short of a time,
half an hour.'

01/10/99   11:00 p.m. I get a big, teddy bear welcome from Eva! Over the
summer she had started calling me mama. I was her favourite. In
a strange way, I was flattered. She warned me that the next time
I came to visit she may have a new mama, a new favourite. I
suppose this is how she deals with the death of her mother.

I am exhausted after twenty-four hours on the night train. Vlasto and Vlado and Maruska are at their usual table. Marcela's loose white ponytail looks really dirty. She takes it off. The gypsy salesgirl is here. The woman offers her a new one. She lets her try it on. Marcela's pimps have to approve every purchase. Marcela looks great in the new hair. She glances at Maruska hoping for her approval. Katja jumps in, saying Marcela looks really great in it. Maruska argues that she doesn't like it.

'If I don't like it the first moment I see it, it's no good. And besides, anytime we buy something new for Marcela to wear, business goes bad.'

The gypsy salesgirl makes faces behind Maruska's back. She wanders around the restaurant impatiently. She pulls out new items from her bags: lip liners, eye pencils and sneakers. Maruska tries on a blue dress with a white collar and white buttons. It makes her look like Minnie Mouse. It's amazing to see how women can transform themselves. They become new people just by changing their clothes. This is the only freedom they have. Whether they are pimps, hookers or office girls. Radek tells me gypsies are very superstitious. Katja says they buy a lot for themselves and their girls but then tuck it away. Later in the evening I see the dress and blond wig still wrapped up in plastic on a chair in the kitchen. Marcela's new hair.

Miluse

In Sokolov, 30/07/99

ANN-SOFI I would like to know how old you are? What is your name and date of birth? **MILUSE** My name is Miluse. My maiden name is Pavlova. I was born 20 January 1951.

What sort of jobs have you had? I worked in a factory for fifteen years. I was a big Communist. I went to political schools in Prague, Moscow and Leningrad.

Are you still a Communist? It was a better life back then. I'm still a member of the party. I still have my card. I haven't given up. One day it will come back again.

What did it mean to be a Communist in this state? There were advantages for my kids. It gave them advantages in school, learning professions and getting into universities. There were benefits if your parents were Communist.

When did you have your first child? I had my first child at eighteen. It was a boy. Milos is his name. Within two years, Zusana was born. Then Honza and Yveta. She died. I was married at the time. Then I got divorced. I was single for six years after that. Then I remarried. I married a Cuban man. I had three kids with him.

What was life like back then? It was very bad because the Cuban guy left the kids and me. I didn't get any child support. Not from him or the state. That was already after Socialism. I had no work. I walked the streets to support my kids.

Do you remember the moment you decided to do that? I made the decision when I realized there wasn't bread for the kids. No flour, nothing.

How did you initially start? Did you have any friends who walked the street? I asked a friend who I knew didn't receive any support but always had money. I asked her how she managed. She told me she walked the street. So I decided to go with her one day and give it a shot.

Can you remember how you prepared yourself? Oh, yes. I remember very well. It was a very strange experience. I had never done anything like that. I mean, I had regular sex at home but I didn't know how to act on the street ... what to say ... what they would want me to do ... so, I asked my friend these questions.

Do you remember your first client? Oh my God, it was horrible. He wanted me to do something I had never done in my life!

What was it? He wanted a blow job without a condom. I said, 'without a rubber, no way.' I had to throw up after. It was horrible.

How much did he pay you? He gave me 50 marks. Plus an extra 20 because he said I was good at it. I told him about my kids and so on. But then I told my friend I couldn't do it and went home.

And after a couple of days what happened? No, the second or third day I went out again. I met this Slovak guy who took care of my girlfriend. I was with him for seven years. But he treated me badly.

How badly? What happened? Well, he said I had to start working for him. I got beaten up ... I had wounds all over.

Do you think he loved you? I thought so at the beginning. Then he started drinking. He was vulgar with the kids. He even beat them up! The police had to get involved. It's gone to the Commission. I'm curious how it's going to turn out. I had many problems with him, I still do. But it's not as bad anymore. He started locking up the food and wouldn't give the kids any and they told me. He was the cause of many problems.

What did he do to the kids? He beat them up. He called them whores!

Do you think he used them? I think he wanted them to walk the street. I said no way. He didn't use them sexually.

How old were your children then? My youngest is fourteen and my oldest seventeen.

I mean back then. Oh ... thirteen and fifteen! It's not that long ago. About a year. Two weeks ago we had some trouble with him.

He comes over and what happens? He kicks the door or climbs through a window. He throws stones at my daughter and calls her a whore. She was afraid to go to school.

Where does he live? Everywhere and nowhere! The police called him in for questioning. I don't know how it will end.

Do you think you can protect your girls from prostitution? I'm positive. We talk about it a lot since I'm in the business. They've seen the types of problems we have. We talk about it very openly. I'm very strict with them. I don't want people pointing at them saying, 'Look, they are like their mother!'.

Do your neighbours know you? Yes, they know me. They also recognize me from street walking.

Does that matter? Well, nobody has said anything so far. They understand if the kids need food I have no other choice. I don't talk about those things with them.

Have you had encounters with the police? I didn't have any trouble with them. They'd check my papers. Once we had a problem and I had to pay a fine.

When did you decide to stop? I met my boyfriend, that German guy [Klaus]. We met on the street. We talked about everything. I told him about my problems with the Slovak guy. How he beat me up if I didn't make enough money. So, we decided to stay together. He became my steady client at the pension. Then the Slovak said 400-500 marks isn't much for a German. I said it was enough for the kids and me. So we got into a fight. He beat me up because I didn't cash in more from the German. Then I kicked him out and the problem started.

When was that? About four months ago. The German guy [Klaus] said he'd give me money but he doesn't want to see me on the street. He'll check on me. If he sees me out there again it's over.

How long did you walk the street? Nine years!

This happened when the Iron Curtain came down? And what happened after that? It started with them saying, 'You are a Communist; you can't work here anymore!'.

What about your girlfriends? Do they still work at the factory? If you were a Communist you had to go. If not, you could still work there.

Do you still meet any of your old friends? Yes. We meet once a year and talk about everything - our problems. I never told any of them what I did. Sometimes they might say, 'hey, we saw you on the street', but I always said, 'come on, it wasn't me'. Sometimes when I met my boyfriend at the pension he'd see all the wounds on my body and he'd get very upset.

Is your boyfriend married with kids? No, he's divorced. He has four kids. The oldest boy is twenty-eight. The youngest girl is eleven. He pays child support for her.

What does he do for work? He paints and wallpapers apartments.

Did you have any bad experiences on the street that you would want to talk about? Yes, I did ... one guy wanted to cut my throat. He had a knife in his car. A German guy.

Can you tell me exactly what happened? I said we should go to my place. He preferred his place – the car. Afterwards he paid. Then he locked me in the car and started attacking me with a knife. I fought back. He started ripping my clothes off my body. I was lucky I made it out of the car. I was almost naked. He took back the money he paid me. I never carried money on me. I always hid it in a ditch next to the street. I put my money in cigarette boxes and hid them in a ditch next to the road.

What did he say? What made him do that? He said he was taking revenge on me as he had on other girls. At that moment, I thought of my daughters. I don't know, maybe some girls hurt this guy in some way. Or, I don't know what happened.

Were you afraid to go back on the street? I was afraid. But the Slovak guy beat me again. I had to go back on the street.

Why do you think the Germans come here to pick up women? Because a Czech whore is a cheap whore. That's what a German friend told me. I mean, the gypsy girls go for as low as 20 or 30 marks.

What do you think of gypsy women? There's not much to say about them. They mess up the business for the other girls. And they're filthy.

Is there competition between the prostitutes? Can you give an example? Well, some time ago the Germans were going to the gypsies, but not anymore. It's very seldom a German goes to a gypsy these days. They steal and they're filthy. There are fights between the white women and the gypsies because the gypsies are being pushed back.

Some gypsy pimps have white women. Isn't that right? Yes, they do. But mostly Ukrainians and Bulgarians!

What do you think of pimps? What kind of men are they? Do they have any self-confidence, or what? They only think about money. Money, gambling machines and gold. The pimps mostly try to impress each other with who has more gold and so on. Often the girls on the street eat only bread and water. If they don't do their job they don't get anything to eat. If you don't go to work you get beaten up. They force the girls to stay on the street until they make a certain amount of money, even if it takes them twenty-four hours.

Do you know women who work without pimps? If a girl is smart she'll say to the pimp, 'Listen, my guy is hiding back there. You better back off if you don't want to get hurt.' It doesn't have to be true. But that only works for a time. My guy was often home drunk. I didn't know what he did to the kids. He only came to pick up the money.

So you gave everything to your pimp. Yes, I used to, not anymore.

How exactly do the pimps force girls to work for them? They give them drugs. You see those girls who are always tired? They're given all kinds of drugs in their food. They really get wasted on drugs. I know girls who are even on dope. I tried drugs too. I was physically down. Working was too much for me. I'd get up in the morning, get up at night, work around the kids ... it was just too much. I told this girl I was always tired and she said here's something to put up your nose. I sniffed it and I was OK.

You could still take care of your kids while you were on drugs? Well, you take your dose and you're OK. Sometimes I'd collapse. I'd sleep through a whole day and I was OK. I managed with the kids but it was tiring.

Did you hear of women being sold to the West or see stuff like that? Yes, I've seen that. They sold girls. The pimps came and said, hey listen, we're going to buy your woman.
The pimps were Czechs, Ukrainians and Bulgarians. They sold me too! To a German! He drove me to Jachymov where some Germans bought me. They wanted me to work for them in Germany. But before we went to Germany they said I had to make them the money they paid for me. They watched me with the first car and I gave them the money. I explained to the second client I had been stolen and had children at home. He drove me back home. And that was that. I didn't go back on the street.
I met them again a long time after that. I told them they must have had me confused with somebody else.
I cut my hair short so I'd have a different hair-style.
They also took my passport. I went to the police and told them I lost it.

The women who are taken to Germany, do they ever come back?

No, they don't come back. They wind up somewhere in Turkey and so on.

What happens to them in Turkey? I don't know! All I know is a Turk wanted me to go to Turkey. I said I didn't know where to leave my kids. He said it would only be a half year but I told him I couldn't do that.

What was it like for you to be a hooker and the mother of three kids? Were you disgusted with yourself? I had to go on the street because the kids needed to be fed. There was nothing that could have been done. At home I cleaned up, washed and cooked for the kids. I was disgusted when the Slovak guy would jump on me and say, 'Show me what you did to the Germans.' I'd tell him to get lost. On top of that he'd be drunk. That disgusted me. He wanted me to do what I did to the Germans. It doesn't work like that. You come home worn out from the street. Standing around all day and night, in the dark, and he jumps on me at home. I was really disgusted. My older kids who are married didn't like what I was doing. But they never said anything against the fact that I walked the street.

Did they try to help you? They have families of their own. See, these days everyone's trying to make things work for themselves as best they can. They're happy I'm with this German guy now and I don't have to walk the streets.

Do you still have the feeling that you were or are a hooker? No. Let's put it this way, some people see me, or saw me, as a prostitute. For me, it was an emergency. I had to feed my kids. Once I had an accident at home … as long as my doctor didn't know I was a hooker she took care of me. The moment she realized, she said she didn't treat prostitutes and sent me away.

Was she a gynaecologist? No, no. She was a normal doctor. I had burned myself.

How did you burn yourself? The boiler in my home exploded. I burned myself with hot water. Anyway, I got into a fight with her. I got upset. I asked her how much money she makes. I told her to guess how much I make. She said she made 12,000 to 13,000 Korunas a month. I told her I could make that on the street in a week and I took off. She had started picking on me.

Have you met her since then? No, no. She tries to avoid me.

Why don't doctors want to treat hookers? What's behind that? They're disgusted. She told me to my face that she was disgusted with me because I walk the street. God knows what I did with those Germans.

My next question might sound a bit funny. What was it like when a client used a condom and you weren't aroused? Did it hurt? What was that like? I mean, I was never aroused. A hooker sees it as a job, an obligation. You know. Come on, quick and bye-bye. Sometimes it hurt. When I had sex with three, four or ten men I'd have stomach pains and all that. And when you have your period the girls use sponges. They don't use tampons … it hurts with that.

What do the clients say when you have your period? Do they still go with you? Yes, they do. Some prefer it. I don't know why. Maybe it arouses them. Some asked if I had it or whether he's the first one that day. One even told me, 'If I'm the first one I'm not going to sleep with you. I'm only going to lick you. If I'm the second I'm going to sleep with you.'

Is it like that when the girl's a virgin? No, no. Whether he's the first guy that day. He said he doesn't get anything from it if he's the first one. If there were more guys before him then it's better. They even pay for that. They pay for that kind of sex. I don't know what they get out of it.

Did you have to pretend to orgasm with each client? Sure, of course. Some want you to moan. Some want you to bark like a dog. Each client is different.

Do the men want to know if they're good? Yes, of course. I'd always say, 'Yes, you're very good.' What can you say, right?

Did life on the street change you, your personality in any way? It was a change because everybody wanted to make love in a different way. Since I've been with my boyfriend I can be myself again. I don't have to pretend anything.

And with your German boyfriend [Klaus], do you have fun with him? Yes, it's normal already. We are like husband and wife. He trusts that I won't go back on the street.

Was there anything positive about your life as a prostitute if you compare it to your life before? During Communism and after? When the Communists were in power there were more advantages for single mothers. We got money from the National Committee, the Region and the Welfare Office. Women didn't have to prostitute themselves. Nowadays, single mothers are poor even if they walk the street. They are forced to walk the street to feed their children.

Do you have anything positive to say about your life as a prostitute? I hung on to my children. I have a handicapped son, Sergei. He is fifteen years old. Mentally, he's like a nine year old. He didn't walk or speak until he was six. So I live for him. I live for my children. But especially for him [Sergei]. He will stay with me forever.

Do you have a question for me? I don't know … I don't know.

What kind of work do you do at home? I saw you doing some work yesterday. It's dirty work. It pays poorly but it's money. It's some sort of padding for cars. For 1000 pieces you're paid 50 Korunas. Even though he [Klaus] gives me money, everything can't depend on him. He's also got expenses.

So the whole family helps with that? Yes, the whole family does it … the whole family.

What do you think of Vaclav Havel? What do I think of Vaclav Havel? He's like a worn coat inside out! One moment he's like this and one moment like that. I believed in Dubcek. He was great. He could have been good.

Has anything improved in the Czech Republic? Everything was so controlled... It was better before. Actually, single mothers and elderly people were better off before. Here's the point: Czechs, or Communists, were stealing, but in small amounts. Prices rose in pennies. Now, they raise prices in larger amounts. I have to pay 2000 Korunas for my apartment plus 700 for electricity. That's 2700 Korunas. How do I buy coal? How do I buy wood? Where do I get that kind of money? I only get 2900 Korunas to support the kids. I also have to pay for the kids' school and things. For two years we didn't have electricity. I didn't have the money to pay for it.

How did you manage? The TV ran on a car battery. I did the laundry by hand. And I had candles and petroleum lamps.

How did you cook? On a wood stove? No, not on a wood stove. I had a little gas cooker.

Thank you for telling me your story. Do you have any questions? How do you think your life will continue? What are your plans? He [Klaus] has plans. He would like to marry me, but...

And stay here? No, we would go to Germany when the kids finish with school. He's nice. He trusts me. You saw him...

Would you like to say anything else? Something you think people ought to know? I would like to say that I don't want any girls walking the street for pimps. They should live for themselves. Go to work or just stay on unemployment. Girls should never get addicted to drugs and prostitution.

Would you mind if I looked around to get an idea how you live? Yes, you can. It's not a problem. It's a bit messy because I'm working on that job.

My house is also chaotic. I'll show you my work. It's a tough job. My hands are dirty from the oil. I have blisters.

Can I ask her some questions? Renata.

You go to school? No, she finished already. She went to school to become a cook or waitress.

Can you get a job as a waitress? Let her answer. No, there's no work. That's why she's doing this.

How did you feel about your mother being a prostitute? What did you think about it? She didn't have a problem with it. She knows I was forced to do it so we could eat.

Can she answer herself? Renata, answer!

RENATA What?

You're supposed to answer!

RENATA What can I say when you always talk for me?

Do you ever think you might do it?

RENATA No.

What would you like to do?

RENATA I want to do what I studied in school.

Even if you have to move far away to get a job? To Prague even?

RENATA I don't know.

Klaus

In Kynsperk, 30/07/99

ANN-SOFI What is your name and how old are you? **KLAUS** Well, my name is Klaus and I am forty-nine years old.

What is your profession? I am a machinist.

Are you married? I am divorced.

Were you married once? I was married twice.

Do you have any kids? Yes, from the first marriage and the second. They are all grown up.

Do you remember what happened when the Wall came down? Yes, I can. At first, life went on normally. Then everything changed a bit. There was no unemployment.

Then what happened? What happened?

Yes, when the Wall came down. Work continued at the factory. But, financially, it became senseless to work there. I started at a West German company, at Volkswagen. I drove a big tractor. I wound up working in construction for a guy from Saarland. At the end I was well, my boss was my brother-in-law.

Were you a Communist? No, no.

Why? Why? It was not my thing.

Is she [Miluse] a Communist? Yes, yes, she was a member of the party. I mean, she was ... that's all over. I never had a desire to be a part of that.

I have a question. When was the first time you picked up a prostitute? Were you married then? I was divorced. It was after my second divorce.

What year was that? Hold on ... it was '93.

From whom, or how did you hear about Eastern European

women prostituting themselves? From whom? It was a very stupid thing. Usually, you can't talk about this with anybody. I had never been with a prostitute in my life. I was getting health treatments for four weeks at a place close to Brambach. Many times we drove there in the afternoons, to eat or to buy cigarettes. I saw it. When I was back home I thought, 'what the fuck?', I'm getting divorced! Honestly, I have to say, the first time I went to a prostitute I just stayed with her.

What do you mean? I stayed with her for three-quarters of a year … I mean, we lived together.

Was she Czech? She was Slovak!

Why didn't it work out? First of all, she was too young. Secondly, we weren't good together.

What did it feel like driving around looking at those women? Now?

No. I mean then. Well, if you drive and look … there are some you could say are … good … beautiful … but many aren't worth stopping for. I'm not interested in how a prostitute dresses. She can dress like a whore or a little bit, she's still a whore. You know what I mean? I'm sure a lot of them make more money when they don't dress like whores, like some of them standing around in high heels. Honestly, I wouldn't step on the brake no matter what. No way!

Do you like it when they dress like housewives? Not like housewives, but like normal women. Otherwise, I'm not into it.

Young women, old women, does that make any difference? No, it doesn't make a difference, actually.

When you stop your car, what do you ask the women? That was never a problem. Honestly, they were all over the place. As a man you didn't have to ask anything.

They did all the talking? Yes, but her [Miluse] ... I didn't meet her on the street.

Where then? In a pub.

But you knew she was a prostitute? Yes, I knew it. Yes, yes. But after a while I would never have thought that they are worse than regular women. I mean, if I look at someone else, you know? I mean, a regular woman.

I don't think I understand exactly what you're saying. They are extremely jealous! When you are together daily, you can't even look at another woman. That is sort of a problem.

Have you spoken with other men about prostitution? What do they say? I have many friends, Germans, whom I know very well. They have it different! Many of them are married with kids, they're older guys, looking for something younger. But that's not my thing.

How old was the youngest prostitute you've seen? On the street? Well, if my guess is correct, thirteen. I know one girl in Kynsberg, she started at thirteen. She has a family now. You can tell these girls are thirteen.

Do you or your friends like the younger girls? No, that's not my thing. That's the reason it didn't work out with that first prostitute. I have to tell you honestly, I turned red every evening going to bed with her. She was the same age as my oldest daughter.

Yes, I suppose that would come to mind. Of course, in the heat of the moment it doesn't enter your mind. But back at home you start to think about it.

You're saying the Germans treat Czech women a bit like.. They are only merchandise! Only merchandise!

An object! Exactly. As cheap as possible!

I heard a lot of men prefer to do it without a condom. Do you do it like that with your girlfriend [Miluse]? With the first one, when I got to know her I thought I'd be better off using a condom. I don't intend to live for a hundred years but I don't want to be destroyed by certain diseases. When I started seeing my present girlfriend it was the same. And now it's not a problem.

Do you think men generally do it without a rubber? I'd say 90 per cent are trying it!

Why is prostitution so big here? Why? That's simple. For the women, it's work! You know what a woman's salary is around here? A salesperson, if she gets 4000 Korunas, that's good.

Do you understand how pimps work? Understand? The question is a bit ... well, I never really understood them. I know that 80 per cent of the hookers have pimps. When a girl makes 50 marks, 30 goes to the pimp. Otherwise, they wouldn't drive Ferraris!

Did women tell you about their pimps? If so, what kinds of stories? She [Miluse] - my woman - never had a pimp ... maybe a long time ago, when she started. She always worked on her own, privately. That's very dangerous.

Did any of the other women talk about their pimps? The first one didn't talk about him and I didn't ask. At the beginning of our relationship I had to live with it! I must say, honestly, she was ashamed to go to the bank to exchange the money she made. So I went for her, every second or third day. When times were good it was 400-450 marks. Well, for a Czech woman that's a lot of money. You can't blame those women for what they did.

Do you know how many prostitutes you met? All in all, probably four. As I said, when I picked up the first prostitute I ended up staying with her for about nine months. When it was over, I met another one. She was not from the street.

So where did you go? A nightclub!

Did you rent a room? No, no ... I took her for the entire night. She came to my house, here on the bed. No problem.

Did you see her pimp? Yes, Wasak. I know him.

You know him? Yes, I know him.

What is he like? He's a gypsy.

Is that good or bad? Well, good or bad ... it pissed her off to work for him. But that's how it works on the street. Everything's divided into regions. If your girl comes into my region we have a problem.

Where are you working now? I'm unemployed. Next month I'm gonna go again ... I'll do what I did before.

What do you think is the most difficult part for the women who walk the street? Not only those who walk the street but also women who work in nightclubs. Women who do it for a long time start drinking or popping pills. That's the worst. Now she [Miluse] has a son and his wife is also in the business.

She walks the street? No, she works in a club! Anyway, she has to go to bed early because she has two clients in the afternoon. But, as I said, they have to take either alcohol or pills. Otherwise they can't stand it. It's not a normal life for these women.

Did you ever have the feeling you used these women? Used ... I mean from my point of view ... no!

Why do married men who have wives to have sex with desire prostitutes? Is there something the wives don't do? Eventually, yes. I realized, the Germans that I know, who are my age or older, have wives the same age. Sometimes they want young blood. And maybe they'll do things the wives don't do! I don't know. I don't know their women.

If men talked more with their wives, would it be different?

Possibly. I'd say if married couples talked to each other more ...
some problems would definitely go away! That's my opinion!

Are men and women on the same level? Sure, why not ... I mean,
definitely! She does the housework ... I try not to get in the way ...
A lot of people don't see it like that!

Do you think a marriage can be like a prostitute with her client?
Eventually it can be but it depends how they get along and their
attitudes. Often it's the man who goes to work and brings home
the money. The wife takes care of the household and the kids.
That's work too but many people don't understand that. They say
it's my money, I earn it ... but the wife who runs the household ...
they say that's not work.

Do you think that men's and women's sexuality are different?
Men go to prostitutes but among women that's not so common.
For a man it's easier!

Why? Because you just jump in the car and drive through the
streets. When you're a German it's no problem because there are
enough of them. Do you understand? For a woman it's more
difficult ... or have you seen any men standing around?

What's the difference between a man's sexuality and a woman's?
Difference, hmm ... for a woman it's more complicated ... to tell
you honestly. I've never been a woman in my life, I don't know
how they feel. I can only see things from my point of view. But
are there any differences? I doubt it sometimes. There are definitely women in Germany who'll marry a man for his bank account.

Is that prostitution as well? Definitely. There's no difference. If it
wasn't for his bank account she wouldn't look at him.

Is prostitution more intense in Eastern Europe? I'd say it's
definitely worse here. In Germany, the Government's more
against it. Here ... nobody cares ... absolutely nobody. Sometimes
I think the Government allows it because that way one doesn't
have to pay customs. That's my opinion, I might be wrong. One

day the cops pass by ... another day they take them with them and then they let them go again. It doesn't make any sense. I heard the Czech unemployment office provides work for women in the clubs.

Really? No! Yes! That's what I heard ... if they are young and good-looking they get a job in a club. I must say, the nightclubs are cleaner. Working outside on the street is the lowest. When it's -30° C outside and you do it in a car, where does she wash herself? Nowhere! That's disgusting.

Did you ever feel lonely? Yes, or I wouldn't have driven out here back then!

Is it difficult to meet German women? No, I wouldn't say difficult. It's not difficult. But, it's definitely more difficult than here.

Why do you think that is? One goes out more here. Where do you go in Germany? Discos, bars ... why would you even go there when all you find are boring vegetables?

Did you ever consider becoming a pimp? No!

Why? It's not my world. I have to tell you honestly, I don't like those guys!

What type of men become pimps and why? You mean, how do they become pimps? That's very simple! I mean, how should I say it? The girl belongs to the pimp already. Do you understand what I mean?

No. First he's her friend, lover, or whatever you want to call him. Then he gets her to work for him. That's how it works!

But how do the pimps get the women on the street? They have them. I mean, really have them. If she doesn't obey he treats her badly ... very badly.

Did you ever talk to any pimps about that? No, never!

Why not? Because I don't want to end up in a ditch here in the Czech Republic. I don't want any trouble. It doesn't sound nice but that's the way it is. It's the same here, like in Germany. A very tough business! No mercy!

Are you afraid of the pimps? Nooo! I'm not afraid ... in Germany it's more difficult for them. They would ask the guy right away what he does for a living. A regular job couldn't afford him all that. He has a Ferrari, he has this, he has that! Here, nobody cares. I mean nobody. I think the pimps pay off the cops. I don't know, but I'm pretty sure of it.

The police get money from the prostitutes and their clients? The police are not only after money.
I've realized when I've passed by in my car and a beautiful girl's standing around and the cops are right next to them, it's fun for them. So, it's not just money.

When you went to a prostitute for the first time, did you have any moral judgements about it? There wasn't much feeling there. I passed her four times before I stopped.
Honestly, after the eighth visit I felt so stupid about the whole thing. See, I didn't know at the time ... but there's definitely something weird about it.

Were you afraid? No, I wasn't afraid. She was kind of nice. I took her to dinner afterwards.

Did it ever bother you that these women had other men before you? Yes, well, that question is cute! If I got to know a normal German woman ... my own age, I would not be her first guy either. It's sort of the same thing, if you see it from that point of view.

Does it feel good to pay for sex? For the man? Well, I wouldn't say that but it isn't a problem. See, if a man in Germany is married, he might look for a mistress and that could get him into trouble. With a prostitute there's never a problem! See, a girlfriend might come stand at your front door. The prostitute would never do that!

What are your future plans? Are you going to move in together [with Miluse]? If it continues the way it's going, I don't see why not. We're close in age, and let's face it, a woman of her age, in that business, doesn't have much of a career left. Let's be honest right? It's like that...

Do you want to live in the Czech Republic with her? Sure, why not? I can work in Germany and live here. It doesn't make sense to move to Germany now because of the kids. Her older daughter is seventeen, she'll have a husband soon. The other one is fourteen, she's still in school. In Germany she would have to start all over again ... in the first grade!

Do you think prostitutes are better than regular women in bed? I wouldn't say that, no! Let's say you don't live with her ... it's business, that's why she does it. I'd say sometimes it's worse than with a normal woman.

Yes? Worse? Yes, worse! She does it for the money! You know ... she's not up to it! For God's sake ... what do you expect?

They must learn some tricks, don't they? They all know a couple of tricks! But if you're married and it works pretty well, the wife knows a couple of tricks too. I'd say it's normal.

I heard Bulgarians prefer to marry prostitutes because the sex is good and they're good housewives. Well ... it has nothing to do with being Bulgarian. There's a saying in Germany, 'the biggest whores make the best wives'!

Is that what the men say amongst themselves? Yes, yes. That's the saying in Germany, 'the biggest whores make the best wives'. They've had their wild times.

Is somebody back? No, no, no! That's her [Miluse's] older son. He works too. His wife works in a nightclub. They're married.

He's got a regular job? Yes, and she works in a nightclub. She earns three times as much as him.

She makes more than him. Do you think he says no to her money? It's possible! He's Czech, he'd be stupid to do that! Nobody does that around here. I gotta tell you, I know guys who live with street prostitutes for five years and these women love their men. It's not a problem for them. She walks the street like it's a normal job. They know how to separate it. In Germany, they say, 'service is service and liquor is liquor'.

Why did you divorce your second wife, or both? With my first wife it was my job, I was away too much. And my second wife, this was after the Iron Curtain came down, I worked 450 kilometres away. I'd come home Friday night and leave Sunday night.

Was it her decision to divorce or yours? I wanted the divorce because I didn't like coming home and finding a guy sitting on my sofa.

What was that? You know, when I came home from work on a Friday night there'd be a guy sitting on my sofa ... I don't like that!

Oh, she had another man, I understand! Well, you know ... what could I do?! There's nothing you can do about that.

Life goes on, right? It must go on. Somehow it always goes on.

OK. Thank you for your time. Not a problem.

Do you want to say anything else to the camera? Well, what more is there to say on the subject? All I can say is, it's very sad! What other perspective do these girls have?

Eva
Motel Hubert, Dubi, 02/08/99

ANN-SOFI I want to ask you some questions. Can I start now?
EVA I just hope I won't be nervous and turn red. I'm already that, I'm sure.

What do your parents do? My father is a soldier. My stepfather is a policeman. And I don't have a mother anymore. I can tell you about it, but I just don't know where to start.... Should I say how he came home and beat her up? And how he did it? Or what? I'll start like this: My father never drank.

Your real father or stepfather? My real father. And my real father had not been home for half a year. He started to cry because it was his birthday. He complained that my mother was no longer with him. Yeah, my mother got beaten up then; he simply beat her up. My stepfather also got beaten up. He is still in the hospital.

But how? With his hands or what? With his hands, but also whatever was in his hands. For example, a briefcase, when he came back from work. But this is only what I heard. He hit her on the head with his briefcase, which was made of iron. Or with whatever was lying around. My father simply loses it sometimes.

What did you do when this happened? What did I do? I was here. I got a telegram. They didn't want to let me go there. But I simply took off. I went to Slovakia and returned after a week. What happened after doesn't matter. The important thing is that I went there.

What did you do when you went back to Slovakia? Well, nothing. I arranged everything for the funeral. Then I was just sitting and sitting or reading a book. I didn't do anything, nothing. I didn't even eat.

So your mother died when your father beat her up? When he beat her up he hit an artery. She was at the hospital for a week, almost two weeks. And then she died.

Why do you have a broken tooth? It happened when the gypsies beat me up.

How old were you when you got into prostitution? Hey, should I tell you everything about it now? It was like this. When I was younger my father was beating us up. So I ran away from home. I was only thirteen or fourteen when I ran away from home, and when I ran away the last time, like always, he locked me up for a month or two once he found me. And I could not get out of the house. And before my eighteenth birthday, the day before Christmas Eve, the 23rd of December, I ran away from home in the evening. He was asleep. I ran away again, and I returned home on the 18th of February. And on the 19th I got locked up. On the 14th of May I had my birthday. I turned eighteen. I was home for three days. Then my father came home and threw me out. He told me he didn't want to see me anymore. I had finished school already, so I lived at my girlfriend's for two weeks. It was her neighbour who told me, 'Come with me! We'll go to the Czech Republic!'. I knew what we would do there, but I told myself, 'So what?'. The neighbour said, 'You'll like it. And, if not, you can go home.' She lived with a gypsy, and you know how they are. They beat you up. He started to beat me up too. And I was here in Dubi for about one year.

Have you been here in Dubi since then? No, I ran away from here. To Slovakia. Me and that girl. It took four days to get there.

You walked there? No, I went by train. But I stopped here and there. I wanted to see Prague, so I hung out there. Then my girlfriend came. A German wanted to buy me from her. He was supposed to pay her 10,000-15,000 marks, and you know how the gypsies are, they see money and they simply need it! So she started to threaten me. So I had to go back. I had to go back. And when we got back, they beat me up terribly. My hands were broken. My legs were broken. I ended up in hospital. When I came back from the hospital, the German got drunk and drove me to the border. He paid for me but then the gypsies took me back. The gypsies told me that everything would happen at the border. When we got to the border, I told him [the German] I must go to the bathroom. The gypsies followed us. Then they drove me back.

When you first came here, what did the gypsies tell you to do?

You had never done this before… When I came here, the girls standing on the street turned around. He told me, 'You'll learn it in two or three days. You'll just be there. You'll do exactly the same as them. Try your best.' If we didn't make 300 marks a day it was a problem. So I did everything I could for that. We simply had to steal 300-400 marks a day. It didn't matter if the client went with us or not.

What did you think in the beginning when all this was happening? Do you remember what you thought? I thought he would tell me to go home after two days. I thought that if I didn't like it, I would just go. But the very first day they called us names. There's a whole family of Slovakian gypsies there. They fight with each other. Somebody makes more money and they get angry and argue with each other. All the time.

What was the trick? And how did you steal money from the clients? I know it's bad! It's like this: for example, I had to sit on that German. I must do it like that so he won't notice. Punch him here. Grab him there. It's quite simple.

What is the main reason the pimps beat up the girls? Simply, they live in a big family and they are jealous. And if the girl doesn't make 300 marks a day, it is very bad. It was like that every day. They scream, and when they scream they beat you up. They don't care. Their father died six or seven years ago. They've had this bar now for five years, or six years, something like that. The father died six months after the bar opened up. The bar is named after him. He was playing in some band and so on. It doesn't matter if the gypsy is young or old, if he is fifty or twenty. They all sit there and wait for the girl to bring them money. There are about nine of them there.

What do they say to you? You're blond. They must like that. They don't care if the girl has dark hair or blond. They have white girls and also gypsy girls. And the gypsy who had me lives with a white girl and they work together. When a gypsy finds a gypsy girl who will make money for him, he tries everything on her, to get her. They have to get her, at any price. But when that girl doesn't sleep with him, he beats her. He beats her.

Do you have any brothers or sisters? From the first marriage I
have one sister and two brothers. And from the second marriage
I have one sister and one brother.

Do you write to them? I write to the brother, the older one. But he
has his own family and his own problems. The other brother, we
like to tease each other. Sometimes he sends me something. My
sister probably knows about it. She's heard about Teplice, letters
come from Dubi…

You didn't tell them? The brothers, no. But the sister knows, for
sure.

Does she judge you? Or treat you differently? Yes, a little bit, yes.
About three months ago she sent a telegram, and she told me.
She never says anything to anybody, she's like that. She would
not say anything to her best friend. She tells me, 'You'd better
stay home.' 'Do what you want, but come back.' 'Don't do drugs
and don't do this and that!'.

Do you take drugs? No. Don't look at me like that! No, I don't take
any! Sometimes when we go camping we smoke a joint. But just
a little bit, so we still know what's going on. But I'm not into
that. We have this boss. His name is Michal. He is twenty or
twenty-three years old. I don't know exactly. When he comes to
the bar, and the bartender is shooting drugs … I don't know if I
should be saying this … but I don't care. So he is taking drugs,
and Michal comes in. He wants all our hands on the bar, and he
looks at them. He checks our hands, legs, completely. Some girls
chew something, but he doesn't even like that.

Can you describe the type of men that come to you? The men
who come here are different. I can't really tell, you know. Some
come sober and leave drunk. Some scare me, and some not. They
don't let the Yugoslavians in. Because of me. I had a bad story
with them once. Some are fat, some are slim. What they are
doing and what they want, I can't really tell.

Do you speak with the clients? In the beginning I was a little bit stupid. But now I know. When he's drunk, I don't talk to him. When I was with the gypsies, there was one who was so drunk that it even pleased me because I had to steal from him. And if I have a chance to make some money, why not? I just slip my hand into his pocket, like that!
Now you will stay at least 5 metres away from me, right? I want you to know that I don't do it to my friends!

You work very hard, anyway. Yes, sometimes.

It's not such pleasant work, maybe? That's why I go outside when the bar closes. The money, the Germans, the cars passing by don't interest me much. I have to go outside, just to sit under a tree or something.

Do you have your own room where you live, and another room to use for your clients? One girl has a boy, so they stay in one room. When there are a lot of us, we stay two in a big room. And then we have a room where we go with clients.

Are you still afraid of the gypsies? Because you left them, couldn't they still come after you? I am afraid a little bit. But I have been here a long time. And Michal … the gypsies know him.

When you were beaten up, did you consider going to the police? I wanted to … I wanted to.

And why didn't you? I couldn't. I was scared.

Do you know anyone who has done that? Yeah, a Slovakian girl too. The police drove her to the Slovakian border, and then she went home. But they found her and beat her up terribly, terribly…. Where I am now, they would never hurt me.

You told us before that you do some cleaning sometimes. Ah! You must clean, you know! Your room, where you go with your client, also the bar. We change shifts with Petra, but we have to clean everything. Sometimes we don't want to sleep so we clean up!

How many clients do you think you have a day? As they come … it's different. Some weeks it's bad. I have maybe eighteen a week. Sometimes it's three a day and two days nothing. That's a bad week. As they come here, I have them.

Does it hurt to make love so much when you don't really want to? You can do whatever, when the client is nice. You have to do whatever he wants you to do. You drink together, and then the girl doesn't mind it at all. I have to do whatever he wants me to do. He has the money, he looks good, and so you try to keep him for yourself. So you have to do whatever he wants.

What would you like to do when you get back to Slovakia? I don't know really. I studied to become a waitress. But I don't want to become a waitress, that's for sure. When I go home, I don't think I'll change much, because I don't know. I guess I'll have to save all the money I make.

What are your interests? What interests me? I don't know. When we wake up, I do what I need to do. When we are outside, I play basketball. I like it a lot. I don't go to the swimming pool, though. That's for sure. Or I just sit. Or I run. But when I sit I don't do anything. I just stare into emptiness. Because TV doesn't interest me at all.

Do you read? Yes, but not much. I like to knit.

Do you have steady clients? If you want to know, yes!

Do they call before they come? They call or write.

When do you have to be back at work? Today? I told Michal I am going to Lake Barbora. Yesterday, I started late, after five o'clock. Michal told me it's not a problem. He says, if you want to go, then go. But I have to come back. I am Eva and I am twenty-one years old.

Thank you very much! Do you have a cigarette?

Police

Dubi, 09/02/99

(Driving through the streets of Dubi)

POLICEMAN You can drive with us from here onwards, it's still early. Later the girls will be outside; now they are inside. It's cold now, if it was summer there would be double the amount. This is the hotel, both respectable guests and, of course, the girls.

ANN-SOFI Does the owner come from the city? The owner is a gypsy from Utsi. That place is Yugoslavian. There, you see the traffic sign? That's where they stand. This is the road that children walk to school on. Now there are two or three of them here. Now he has girls here to work and make money for him.

Are the girls high on drugs? Yes, they are. Also the Czech girls, but those from the lower level. And the way they live, it's horrible. They make their business and exchange it for Deutschmarks and then they buy drugs. Two years ago I was in a shop where there had just been a burglary and the thief was still there. We fought, and later, when I had him under control, when I frisked him, I pricked myself on a hypodermic needle. I went for regular examinations and tests. Thank God, everything was clean, but it felt strange. But considering what's going on here, that's nothing.

Are you scared sometimes? I think fear has its place here. Because if we weren't scared we would get hurt more often. Those who went to school at the state police get hurt more often because they think they've learned everything in school – how to fight. But on the street it's different, it's either him or me. Turn left here.

(At the police station)

A crime is a deprivation of liberty. These are portraits according to a woman's testimony. They have been here for a long time, up to three years. We haven't found them. These are children from Slovakia – the same problems with pimps. We have large amounts of photographs that the parents bring to us. They come here to look for their daughters and give us more photos.

Have you found any missing girls? Yes, we have.

What condition were they in? There are different kinds. There are girls who want to work, but change their minds after a while. And there are girls who never wanted to do it. And then, the third kind, who is doing it all the time.

We've heard stories about girls who were locked up in their rooms for several months, who didn't get enough food, who were in a terrible condition. Have you seen any cases like that? Sure. Right now I don't remember anything concrete, but, for an example, there was this one girl who jumped from the second floor, to save herself. It was on TV. The girls get the wrong information – just because their documents are taken away from them they think they are trapped. The girl who wants to escape, escapes. It doesn't matter if she has her documents or not. It has happened that a respectable German brings them here, often they have not even had sex with them. She tells them her story if she knows the language, and they bring her here.

Can you describe the pimps, who they are and where they come from? They are mostly gypsies. They speak Czech; they are a lower class, bad mannered, from a family with fifteen children. This is the only way to make money without working. They start with their sister – it's common that they are pimps for their sisters and other relatives. Or, it is a mother with her children. That's normal. Ten years after the Velvet Revolution ... those children are not children today. Mostly it's gypsies and, of course, Bulgarians. After the raid the state police took sixty people so they almost disappeared. Here you find corpses in the woods. The girl who didn't want to work and got killed. But there are not many Bulgarians here. There are thirty-six bordellos in Dubi. The Russians and the Yugoslavians own a third of them and the rest belong to the gypsies.

Do you remember any case where a mother sold her own children or relatives? That bordello I showed you, there are several cases where mothers are pimps for their own daughters.

Do you know anything about Petko? In my opinion we know a lot, but we don't talk about him. That's a story we don't want to talk about. Nicely put, he had long fingers. Very long fingers!

Were you there when they found the girl? Not me, but my colleague was. They dug someone up.

No one could say if Petko was responsible when they found her. It was simply a corpse. Of course she was found on his property. But he wouldn't even have known, he was surrounded by twenty to thirty people. One thing you can say about him, he was nice to the girls in front of us. He wasn't stupid.

Has he been captured? Yes, they caught him in Poland. But we never had any problems with him. If the girls worked outside, and we told him they couldn't stand there, then they didn't stand there any longer. He also accepted fines. He was accommodating. He was one of the few.

You said you are guarding the school in the mornings. Why? Three to four cases during the past two years where Czech, but mostly Germans, dragged girls into their cars. We got one of them – those old men who drive past the school. When the parents found out there was an outcry! That was three years ago. We had one case of child prostitution, two years ago. A studio was found where they filmed child pornography. A German owned the place; the kids were from here.

What is your personal opinion of prostitution? I don't know, but it exists in all countries; it's the oldest profession. If one could limit it, from here to there, to public houses, it wouldn't be a problem any more. If there was a 'love street' in each city or in the harbours … I've not been everywhere but I've read about such streets and seen pictures. The street goes through the city, so the city is involved in the activity. It's the same everywhere, and unemployment is increasing, and for women that I know have families, they come here once or twice a week to earn a little extra, to buy something for their kids. Also older women come here, fifty to sixty years old.

Do the girls know you since you often drop by? They know us by surname, or even by our first name. They're often here at the police station to sign different kinds of papers, where our names are written. If she reads the papers she knows who brought her in. They often have a good memory.

How come some of your old friends from school became pimps? It's probably the money that's tempting. They have a bad education. They would not have become pimps if they had gone to college. The family background plays a part in it, divorce, for example. I know two guys from Teplice who work as pimps.

How does the population react to the prostitution? Are they used to it or do they protest? Those who live right here are protesting twenty-four hours a day. But the interest in the protest list has cooled off. People who live further away aren't in contact with it. There are problems with the neighbours when the pimps drive home late at night. The biggest problem is the children who have to pass the hookers and people that walk from work. The hookers watch their territory, and they are fully capable of slapping a woman passing by, without seeing that it's just a normal woman on the way home with her shopping. It happened once that a normal woman was chased away because they thought she was a prostitute. A normal woman would have to dress in a sack and ashes to separate herself from the prostitutes. But the street is extreme, the other parts of town are not so bad. It happens that the Germans bring a girl from the street and drive to a dark alley, and the neighbours hear what they are doing, and then people call us and complain.

There are obviously a lot of people who make money renting their houses? The local people don't own any houses here any longer. It's mostly people from Prague, who discovered early on that they were worth something, and today they earn 100,000 Korunas a month. But there are very few locals. Maybe they have a bed and breakfast, but they don't live off the prostitutes. There are respectable travellers as well.

Are there a lot of drugs here? A lot. Teplice is the second largest place after Prague. I've heard students come here to have fun, drink a few beers. Marijuana is cheaper and the effect is the same. But that's the students. I don't think there are drugs inside the bordellos, they would not allow it. But the girls on the street, they are drug addicts, all of them. The Yugoslavs, they are laundry machines for money. He buys a bakery or a lovely restaurant, where he launders his money. I used to work in Teplice, where they use brown Asiatic heroin. Here it's more Perotin. People are skilful, they cook it themselves. There are a lot of people who live from this. Boys are already starting in high school. They can live off just doing deliveries, and they do not even have to sell.

So everything is connected? Yes, the organized crime is connected to everything. Everything is connected and everything exists here. The girls on the street have to stay out all night long, and in -15°C; it's impossible to work like that without drugs. Someone steals a car here, 300 metres down the road they take it apart, another 300 metres further down they're selling the same car in parts.

(Talking to the Chief of Police)

CHIEF OF POLICE Maybe I should sit over there? But I guess it's a rather untypical setting. Maybe it's too idyllic? We aesthetes prefer things like that.
You can do this work in two different ways: either you are a zealous policeman, or, in order to find a balance, you get yourself involved with aesthetic experiences.

Did you choose that painting yourself? The painting was in the office when we redecorated. I am interested in art, my girlfriend is an artist and Dr Kucerova is a well-known painter, she sells quite a lot. I'm interested in music, all those things, because a person who lives in this environment, with the low-lifes of society, has to have his own circle of friends to compensate.

Have you been here a long time? No, only two years and I'll quit in three months. It's because of what's going on in this province.

We have just had elections here. I was so successful in my fight against prostitution that I was fired. My position was cancelled...

Petra
Patio at Motel Hubert, Dubi, 24/08/99

ANN-SOFI First, tell me your name. How old you are. Where you're from. Just your first name. **PETRA** I have to laugh.

Can you repeat that again. My name is Petra. I'm nineteen. What else?

Where are you from? I'm Slovakian.

What was life like before you left home? I lived with my parents. How can I explain this ... I have four brothers, a mother and a father. But my grandparents raised me since I was eight months old. I didn't get along with my mom. That's why my grandparents took care of me.
How do I explain this ... my grandparents were killed. The ones who raised me. First my grandfather. Then my grandmother died too. I was in the hospital. I was pregnant with my daughter. My grandfather went for a walk in the evening and some kids killed him. Young skinheads.

Do you know why? I don't know why. I guess they didn't like something about him. He was seventy-eight. He died almost immediately. They kicked him badly. I called him from the hospital. I had to see him. He took my hand. He wanted to tell me something.
It was hard for me. I loved them more than my mom. They took care of me since I was a baby. They gave me everything I wanted. My mother resented them. I know my mom had problems with my father when I was little. But I can't forgive her. She treated me badly. Me and my older brother. Just me and him. The other brothers were fine. My older brother moved out. He bought an apartment in another town. He doesn't keep in contact with her. She threw me on the floor when I was eight months old. We didn't get along very well.
If you listen to the news you've probably heard of my father. Never good things. My father is the gypsy king of our town. His name is Jan Farkas. Have you heard of him? Yes? Well, that's my dad.

Do you speak Romano? No, I don't. My mother is white.

Does your father know what your doing? If he knew he'd come here with the whole army!

How did you get into prostitution?` I went to a disco with a girlfriend. They just grabbed me. They threw me in a car and drove me here.

What were you doing at the time? At home? I worked in a shop.

Who were these people? How did they approach you at the bar? What did they say? We went to a disco. This passing car stopped. They threw me in and drove away. They were Russian. They drove me here. I didn't want to do this. They beat me – badly. They gave me injections. I ended up in the hospital for a month. I didn't want to do this. But they threatened me.

What did they say to you? Yeah. They didn't say anything. They just grabbed me. After several hours they gave me an injection. I don't remember anything after that. Simply, I was here.

What happened the first day you were here? Nothing happened the very first day. I was locked in a room somewhere. I didn't know where I was. I remember waking up when we crossed the border. I showed them my passport. Then I was here.

What happened after that? After that first day they brought me to the bar. They had me sit in the bar. I didn't want to work. I wouldn't do what I was told. They got very angry. They beat me up. They cut me with a knife. Then they took me to a hospital. I was there for two months. They would come to the hospital sometimes just to cause me trouble. When I got out they sold me.

You were stabbed? Yeah.

Would you show me? Yeah.

That's where they cut you? They also broke my head. I have a scar from that.

Why didn't you tell someone at the hospital what had happened? I couldn't tell anyone. They threatened me. The Russians are like that. Whatever they say, they do. They had my passport and papers. I was afraid if I went home they'd come after me.

The first night, weren't there other girls in the bar you could talk to? There were girls there. There were a lot of girls. They treat all the girls badly. They beat them up a lot. The girls work from six o'clock in the evening to six o'clock in the morning. If a girl doesn't make 500 marks they beat her up. And she has to work again from six o'clock in the morning to six o'clock in the evening.

What happened when you left the hospital? They came to get you? Yeah. They sold me right away. They drove me back to the bar. I worked for a few hours. Then they sold me. This guy bought me.

You were sold to gypsies? Did you live in their home? Yeah.

What was their house like? Were there other girls there too? They had kids. Three small children.

What did they say when you started working for them? You know, they didn't treat me badly. They didn't yell. I wasn't with the guy Marcela's with. I was with another guy. His brother. He was nice. He and his wife helped me a lot. But there were times I had to stand outside all night in the cold.

Did you ever contact your family? Yes, I called home. I wrote home. My family doesn't know what happened to me. They don't know what I'm doing. If they did, they'd kill me.

Did you get paid when you worked for them? No.

Was there a reason why? You know how it is. They don't give money to anybody. When a girl has a pimp or a boss, she doesn't get any money. They'll sell their wives too. When they saw me going to a room with a steady client they assumed he was giving me money. They'd search me afterwards to see if I was hiding anything.

Did you leave this bar because something happened? They went home and left me sleeping here one day. And I just went to the other bar. Now I'm with Michal. He knows I've suffered a lot. He lets me do whatever I want. I can go wherever I want. Michal hates it when girls are beaten up. He's against it. Those guys did come for me. Michal had a gun in his hands. They took off.

Then what happened? Well, now when my ex-pimp sees me he says hello. He talks to me. He had told me before this happened that I could leave. He said I just had to pay back the money he paid for me. But if someone makes a lot of money for you, you don't let go of them that easily.

Last night when you were here the gypsies seemed very angry! Yes, they were angry.

How did you get your passport back? When the Russians sold me they gave the man my passport and papers. He returned them to me. He was scared. He thought I'd call the police. I was his first girl. They didn't know how things work.

What happened to Marcela? Marcela still works for them. She's worked for them for three years.

What do you think of Marcela? Why doesn't she leave them? Marcela's a good girl. If she could, she'd leave. But she can't. That happens. I worked for his brother, you know, the one with long hair, the one who was sitting here with that red haired girl with rubber bands in her hair. They are very different. The other brother's really bad. He and his wife are very bad. She wouldn't dare leave them. They would find her. They would cause her a lot of trouble. They would beat her up. They beat her terribly. Once, when I first got here, it was New Year's Eve, she came to work ... she used to talk to the husband a lot at work. When his wife left him to go visit her home, he accused her [Marcela] of being the reason why. So, he beat her. Kicked her a lot. He hit her head against a table.

Could she work with bruises all over her? Yes. She had bruises all over her body. They didn't care. When she had a fever of 39 or 40 degrees she had to work.

How do the gypsies justify what they're doing? What do they say to her when they tell her why she should... Why do they do it? For the money. For the money.

Have you heard of girls defending themselves? When a girl's in a room it's for a half an hour. Sometimes they'll tell you to stay only for fifteen minutes. But ... you saw the scene when that girl was in the room ten minutes over. They screamed at her. When business is bad and a girl makes only 70 marks, they force her to steal money from the German customers. They forced me too. But I never stole any money from anybody. They were very upset with me. They asked me why I didn't want to do it. But I just didn't want to.

What happened to your girlfriend who was with you at the disco? I don't know. I haven't seen her. I don't know what happened to her. They probably took her somewhere in Germany.

When you were back in Slovakia did you talk to your mother? Or your girlfriend's mother? Yeah. My girlfriend's family found out what happened. I told them. But they didn't say anything to my mom. They announced she was missing. The police are investigating that.

Has she come back? How many years has it been? It hasn't been years. It was about five months ago.

Is the guy you work for now a nice guy? Michal is very nice.

Does he fight sometimes? Katja told us he came here and beat someone up. It was a Bulgarian man. His name is Richie. I told you he [Michal] doesn't like it when girls are beaten up. One day this guy came to the bar. He lost control. There was shooting. He took a shot right next to one of the girls. Michal got very angry. He told the guy to take it outside. But this guy wouldn't stop. He beat up some girls. Michal got very pissed off. He dragged him [Richie] outside. He beat him a lot.

Was the Bulgarian guy a pimp? Something like a pimp. He was part of the Russian Mafia. Michal is very well known in Teplice. Everyone is scared of Michal! Michal's known on the streets here. Did you know that for a week I was with a Bulgarian Guy? His name is Petko! He killed a lot of girls here. He actually wasn't that bad to me. But he wanted a lot of money. The girls made 2 million marks a month for him. He had about thirty girls. He had them in several bars. He started with one girl and slept outside. Then he made it. He made a lot of money. He had contacts in the police department. The police here help pimps a lot. The Dubi police are corrupt. Those girls simply had to do it. They didn't want to, but they had to do it.

Does everybody have a good relationship with the police? Not everybody. Some of them do. Michal has a lot of friends who help him. If the police stop and search us they'll take me somewhere and then drive me back.

What? If the police come here to take us in for questioning they don't take me. They take me to a parking lot. I wait fifteen to twenty minutes. Then they take me back.

Are the police your clients too? After work they come to the bar. Not as clients, as friends.

I'd be interested to know what Michal did before this. He had a billiard hall.

Why are people scared of him? He has very good contacts. Good friends in Russia, Poland, the Ukraine. When they all get together, there are 200 of them.

Do these friends come to the bar? Yeah. If no one pisses him off or hurts him everything is fine. He won't hurt anybody. But if something happens twice he goes after them.

Have you seen that happen? Yeah.

Can you give an example of an argument? It was because of me.

Somebody said something bad to you or...? No. Once a Russian man came in. We're not allowed to go with them to the rooms. He got upset with me. He slapped my face. That's how it started.

Why can't you go with Russian men? When you go with a Russian to a room they can't make up their minds. They try to pick on you. They might beat you. They might do something to you. Like give you drugs and bullshit you. To get you to leave with them. They're like that. They'll come see you several times. They just bullshit you.

The Ukrainian girls? Don't they have problems with the Ukrainian Mafia? Yes, sometimes.

They come here? They come here but they're thrown out.

What do the Ukrainians say when they come? Well, the girls who work here used to belong to them. Before Michal bought them. So they wanted the girls to give them half of what they earned. They threatened them. But Michal took care of it. They don't come here anymore.

How can they ask for money after they sold them? They're stupid. They actually think those girls will give it to them. If it wasn't for Michal the girls would have to give it to them. They'd be forced to.

Did you have any clients yesterday? Yesterday? Yes.

How many? Just one.

What kind of guy was he? A German guy. You remember the German guy with me when you came here? The one I went to the room with? That's him. The young one. He often comes to see me. He wants to marry me. He wants to take me to Germany.

And do what? He wants to marry me. He wants me and my daughter to live with him in Germany.

And what do you say? I don't want to.

He fell in love with you? I guess so.

So what do you tell him? I said no. He was very surprised. He asked why not! I told him I wanted to go home in two weeks. He was quiet. Then he told me he wanted to go with me. He said he wanted to meet my parents.

What about young boys? Do they come here? Boys who have never made love. Have you been with anyone like that? I haven't met anyone like that yet. Eva has. A lot of young Germans, twenty to twenty-five years old, come to this bar. I don't know why. The older men are the steady clients.

Do clients know each other? Some of them. Sometimes groups of friends come. What time is it?

Ten minutes to five. I should go now. If you want to do this again, I could come tomorrow at ten o'clock.

Tomorrow we might go away. But we're staying here until Sunday. Do you have a phone? Yes. I need to recharge it.

OK. You can't call? Yes, I can.

Yes? So, call me. When you wake up. We'll drive up there. We can go swimming. OK.

Thank you. You're very welcome. Can you open the door for me?

Sure I can.

Katja

The office at Motel Hubert, Dubi, 03/10/99

ANN-SOFI How old are you? What's your name? **KATJA** I am twenty-six years old and my name is Katerina.

What did you do after the Revolution? I had a part-time job in a restaurant. Then I worked for the exchange office in Dubi.

What is your family background? My parents are divorced. They both have new partners. We get along very well; we see each other frequently. I have a good family background. I have an older sister.

What does your father do? My father worked as a waiter. After the Revolution he opened his own restaurant, which he has now.

Is that in Teplice? He has a restaurant and a gambling hall in Teplice.

How did you start out in Dubi? How did prostitution develop around here? Dubi was a forbidden place for me. I met Honza at the exchange office. Next door there was a small hotel, converted from a store. I met girls there who rented rooms for sex. You know, beginnings are tough. It's like going to university for the first time – a new place, new people, a tough environment.

Did you study at a university? I just did the tests but I didn't pass. I thought I'd try again a year later but I changed my mind because I had my freedom already. I was financially independent. I'm pretty sure my parents would have supported me, but once you get a taste of freedom it's hard to go back to school, you know.

What type of people came to the exchange office? They were usually German tourists, but also pimps who came to exchange their money. When the Ukrainian pimps moved here, they went there too, because they had money. And also the girls...

So your first contact with the prostitutes was at the exchange office? Yes.

What type of Germans went there? You know, regular people. For example, the couple who came here to buy something. Or German tourists who wanted to exchange their marks for Czech Korunas, because they didn't want to get ripped-off paying with marks at a restaurant.

Were the girls on the street more then? Can you describe that a little bit? Nowadays when you drive around you see all the bars. It used to be that all the girls were just standing outside on the street. Now everything is modernized here. Before you had 200-300 girls standing around.

And how many kilometres is that? How long is the street? I don't know. From the Motorlax up to here it's approximately 2 to 3 kilometres.

Were the rates confusing at that time? When they exchanged their money and paid the girls, was it confusing for them? Do you mean after the Revolution? When Germany united suddenly everything was confusing for them. Is that what you mean? For the East Germans, yeah, it was confusing for them. I remember one German was exchanging his money and didn't know he could have a girl for 50 marks. Especially when they got Western marks.

Was that good for the girls, the prostitutes? Sure it was good. When the girls asked for 1000 marks a night they got it. The Germans didn't really know what was going on here, it was new to them. It's not like that now. When they don't want to pay they try to negotiate the price.

Was that the reason all the girls came to work here? I don't think so. The girls didn't care at all. They came here because they made a lot of money from prostitution. Some of the girls didn't want to be here in the first place. It's not like nowadays when the girls come here to make money because they have kids and stuff. Before they were forced to do it. Nowadays they aren't.

So it was organized from the beginning to bring those girls here for prostitution? Yes.

And who were their pimps? Mostly gypsies. The gypsies started everything here.

And then? And then the foreigners: Yugoslavians, Russians and Bulgarians.

And those people are still here? Yes, we still have foreigners around. But it's different nowadays. There are a lot of bars here now and the girls get a percentage. It's like them working as strippers, you know, for the performance they'd get 200 Korunas. The prostitutes have their rooms and they have their percentage. It's different now.

Who opened the bar next to the exchange office? It was Honza.

You met Honza at the exchange office, and then you got married? Well, we got married after five or six years!

Did he speak to you about opening the pension? That pension only had rooms. There was a small entrance and then the rooms. In the exchange office there was a space where people could drink while they waited. Business grew rapidly, so we decided to make a bar out of the small entrance. That's how it all started. Where the Venezia is now, there used to be a grocery store. We were the only ones here back then, Jecho and us. Nobody else. It was perfect.

And how did the pension work exactly? When the bar opened, Honza already had some friends who told him they would bring some girls over. That turned out to be Maruska and her sister. It started that way ... we opened at seven o'clock. The girls worked and I made money from renting the rooms.

And how many rooms were there? There were two rooms. It was just enough. Back then, it went faster. It's not like that nowadays with all the negotiations. It just went quick, quick. You can figure it out yourself. If a room costs 20 marks and we made 600 marks per room a day. A lot of people used to come here, you can't compare it with today ... I mean, not every day, but on good days.

On good days each girl made about 1000 marks. It wasn't anything special to make that.

What year was that? 1991–92.

Do you still have the same friends you use to have? Has this work changed your life in any way? Not really. I still have the same friends. It doesn't mater if you work as a cleaning woman or as a doctor, I don't think this affects friendships so much. My parents were a bit confused about it. They didn't know what was really going on here. They use to say, 'you work in Dubi, oh...'.

And then you bought this motel? When Honza and I met, he had a girlfriend. They didn't have any children though. We were together almost a year before they separated so it was kind of weird for me. And we were working at the pension. Then we bought this motel which was in really bad condition. First we bought the half where the Red Bar is. We worked for a while and then we started renting it out.

Who did you rent it out to? To Petko.

Can you describe him a bit? What kind of man was he? Petko was a friend of Jecho, the Yugoslavian guy. Jecho and Honza had known each other a long time. So he asked us if we wanted to rent out to Petko. He said he had girls and stuff and when I saw him the first time he looked like a nice uncle. He was small. He acted like a gentleman, he knew I was Honza's girlfriend. Later I heard a few things about him. I saw him in a few situations where he wasn't that nice. But otherwise he acted like a regular guy when you met him. He had nice clothes, good cars, he gave me the impression he was just a regular guy.

Is he Bulgarian? Yeah. He had been renting this place for a long time. Then we started reading about him in the newspaper. He had a lot of nicknames. I really couldn't believe it when we read he was convicted for murder in Bulgaria and actually escaped from jail. It's a paradox. He had escaped from Bulgaria and here in Prague they gave him a work permit and so on. I didn't understand that at all.

He didn't come here alone, right? He came with his mother and kept all these Bulgarians from Teplice around him. I really think Bulgarians, as a nationality, stick with each other. They need a leader to show them the way, otherwise they are lost. He was their leader and he was very good at it.

And what was his mother like? I didn't know her that well. But once I went to the bar and there she was, looking like an Indian woman. Otherwise she looked quite normal. I don't think that she understood Czech very well, she just said, 'good morning', and things like that. She took good care of her girls although they say she wasn't that good to them. I don't believe that. But I am not the one who can really say.

Did they live here also? They had several apartments around here. They lived someplace else but they had apartments here too. They had their girls here with their guards.

When you started reading about him in the newspaper did you have any problems with him? We didn't have a personal problem with him. But when we went to pick up the rent, the guys who opened the door were pointing guns at us. That was kind of scary. I always went with Honza. Simply, it's better not to have any arguments with them. When they opened the door like that, it was their defence. They were scared, or, I don't know.

How long did he actually stay here? And what happened afterwards? He lived here for about five years, then suddenly the police made their strike. We had a restaurant, which was open until ten o'clock, and we had the bar upstairs. They [Petko and his gang] had the Red Bar. One night, around midnight, the police called us and said we had to come to the restaurant. They wouldn't say anything specific. So I called the restaurant next door and the guy told me that we had probably been robbed. So we drove up there and everything had been smashed. It looked about the same as all their [Petko's gang's] places around there. Everything smashed. It happened so fast. We didn't know what was going on. We wound up with our house all smashed up. The restaurant was closed and locked up but the police broke inside and destroyed the place.

There was also something you said before? That happened later when there were other Bulgarians here. The ones you saw. They had some girls and one of these girls made accusations against them. The police came, this time while we were open. They came through the front and back doors and we had some workers in the garden. Everybody had to lay down on the floor and put our hands behind our heads, just like in the movies. The police had a warrant to do this and that. They had this ridiculous behaviour. They acted as if they were onto something big or something.

And you were here alone? It didn't happen at night; it happened during the afternoon.

What did they tell you? How did it end up? They didn't tell me anything. They just said, 'lay down on the floor'. They searched the whole house. They arrested one Bulgarian girl but took us all in for questioning. Like you, they asked me the same questions, 'How long have you worked here? How much do you charge for a room?', and so on. I had a weird feeling because I hadn't done anything. I was scared because I didn't know what was going to happen. Someone may accuse you…

Petko wasn't here at that time, right? This happened after he left. He was arrested with his Bulgarian pals, but actually he escaped. You know, they say only four government officials knew about this [police raid] and him [Petko]. Vanja was with him at the time; they went to Korea together.

What happened to his mother and those girls? They arrested them all. All those girls. And they had to leave the country … actually, four of them, including the mother. The main group was sentenced and Petko received a sentence too, even though he wasn't here. They later caught him in Poland. Some of the girls were let go and they came back here to pick up their stuff.

And Vanja was working here at the time? At this bar? **Vanja was working in Niva. We didn't know each other well. I knew her and she knew me. She had been working for Petko a long time.**

Did you speak with Honza about the arrest? How did you feel about it? **When it happened the first time, when they smashed up our place, they didn't take us anywhere because we hadn't done anything. But they told Honza to calm me down otherwise they would arrest me for contempt. I was upset when I saw the whole place smashed up. I had put so much work into it and the police acted like nothing had happened. So the first reaction was spontaneous and Honza and I spoke about it very realistically. We just thought about the things that needed to be fixed and about preparing all the papers. Honza isn't the kind of person who talks about things like that with me, but we did talk about it later.**

And then Vanja came here? **No, no. Vanja came here later with another Bulgarian, Loro. His brother knew her from Korea. So, that's how they got here.**

And then she started to work on her own? **Yes, but not right away. At first she worked with them, she had to pay him [Loro] off some money. Then she started working at the billiard hall and then here; she made a deal with them.**

Did you become friends with her? **Yes, we became friends but I regret it.**

Why? Is it a problem being friends with the girls? **She disappointed me. It doesn't matter if she is a prostitute or a hairdresser. She disappointed me as a person. She owes me money and she told me that she would come back but she never did, she didn't even call me.**

You have to separate friendship and business. **Yes. Honza can do it but I can't. I am a sensitive person. When I started doing this job and I saw the gypsies beating up the girls, I cried every night for three months.**

Can you describe when the girls are working here and a new girl arrives? Describe what goes on? There aren't so many girls here, so they get to know each other well. There is competition between them, like who makes more money. It's all about money. Marcela, she is like that. She wants to be the best. But it's all about the chemistry between the girls. It's the same thing with schoolmates, some of them you like and some you don't.

A lot of the girls have the same story. They're forced to come here, they're beaten up, then they leave, then they return and become independent. Do you agree that it's like that for most of them? Girls who were forced to come here and are beaten and who manage to get out of it, most of them go back home or to Germany to work for themselves. But other girls need to be beaten. They actually miss it. Those girls are not from good families. They break contact with their families. Gypsies have the ability to manage those girls. Those girls are hooked on it. It's a dependence. They are afraid to be alone.

If you have friends come over who later go with one of the prostitutes, what do you think about that? I had this boyfriend I was with for one or two years. He came to see me even though I was with Honza. He got drunk and actually went with a girl. That broke something inside me. I do have a bad feeling about it. It's weird when I see our customers' wives and speak with them, but you get used to it. It's weird but ... I say they're just men.

Have you changed your opinion of men since you started working here? No, I haven't changed my opinion ... why? Women are like that too. They get drunk and do something. It's better if a husband pays for it ... then he can erase it ... a steady mistress would be much worse. That could break the relationship.

Were you afraid Honza might go with the girls? No, I wasn't afraid. I told him it was like this: when you work as a butcher you don't eat salami because you know what salami is all about. He would be against himself if he did anything like that.

Do the girls confess their problems to you? I don't take their confessions that seriously. I wanted to help Marcela at the beginning when she was beaten up but I realized that she would do it all over again. But also, at the beginning, the girls were afraid I'd tell someone. Now Marcela tells me that she has ironing to do and that she can't sleep. The girls are brainwashed so that they just tell me what they do.

What did you do specifically to help them? Marcela, for example, she came here one evening so badly beaten she couldn't move for three days. They had hit her head against the bathroom faucet. So I got her medicine and we talked and I told her, 'Marcela, I'm not afraid. I'll give them the money or I'll give you the money and you can go home or you can stay here and work.' But when they came for her she went home with them after saying she wouldn't. So I don't take those things seriously anymore. She could have worked for Vanja because Vanja was here at that time. What time is it? I have to go!

There's only five minutes left on the tape. Yeah...

Can you describe your daily routine? You finish here, then what do you do? When I finish work, it's like today. I sleep here a while, then I work and then I go home for a while. When I have the day off I sleep or I have stuff to do at home and things to buy and the accounting. In the evening we have to come here anyway. So we stay a while and then Honza and I go visit some friends or go have a beer somewhere. And then go home. I hate it but I can't be without it. Even on vacation I'm on the phone half the time. Even my father told me I was really into it. Everyone comes to me when they need something, and I like that. It's a good feeling being appreciated. I probably couldn't have a normal job anymore!

What is you timetable? Like at eight o'clock you go to sleep and you sleep until ... when did you go to bed today? 7.30 a.m. The girls still had some clients then? Yes. And I can't just take off. I have to clean ashtrays and stuff like that.

And then you slept? I slept until eleven o'clock, Honza woke me up. It's not like this all the time. Honza has a lot of work right now. Usually he takes me home. But it will continue like this for a while. Whenever there's more work it's like this.

What is the new business you started? A refreshment booth in a trailer. It can move to different locations. I don't believe in it but Honza does it anyway.

What would you like to have happen here with your life? I would love to continue working here but to change it so that we aren't here by ourselves. Dubi will last two more years. Even though he [Honza] doesn't want to, we will be forced to sell. I can't imagine living here if business stopped. I also would like to have a family. I'd like to travel around and slow down. I just can't go on like this. By forty I would be totally burnt out. I still have some common sense.

Thank you very much. You spoke so clearly.

Vanja
Motel Hubert, Dubi, 06/02/99

ANN-SOFI So, how old are you? **VANJA** Twenty-one.

And you come from Bulgaria? Yes I do.

How did you come here? I took a bus, and then I went to Germany through the border district of Cínovec.

What was your reason for leaving and coming here? Did you know what you wanted to do? I knew what I wanted because I've done this work for six years, and I wanted more money. In Bulgaria I didn't have enough money.

Are you in contact with your mother? Does she know what you are doing? When I was stolen and sold the first time, I wrote my mother a letter and told her that I was OK. Then I returned when I was sixteen to pick up my passport. I told my mother I was with a boyfriend and that I was OK. But my mother had heard some rumours about what I was doing. But I told her I wasn't working as a prostitute. My mother said, 'It doesn't matter what you're doing, just come back!'. But I didn't want to, because I saw a lot of money waiting for me.

Can you describe the characteristics of your clients? Mostly Germans. They are dirty. All the time I have to tell them to take a shower, to take their socks off; they chew gum when they make love. I know them, they cannot do anything to me. I do it to them just by hand or with my mouth; they say that I am a bad girl, they pay, and I just say, ' Thank you, thank you, bye'. I know them, the Germans! I also have regular clients who take me for the whole night. They do not only want to make love. When they visit there is drinking, eating, a lot of fun and sometimes we will not make love. They give me gifts and they pay well. For those kinds of men I am able to do that, but for others...

Have you ever had a bad experience, when you were really scared? I am not afraid of Germans. Sometimes Czech guys come, that take narcotics and show their weapons. I don't show it in my face that I am scared, but I am really scared inside.

Did you ever have to defend yourself, or run away? Not any more, I can see at once what kind of character the clients have and how I should talk to them.

When did you begin to feel that this was a good way to earn money? I worked two months for the gypsies, then for two months with a Bulgarian guy; after that with another one who bought me. He let me work for myself, he did not ask me for money.

Didn't he take any money, any percentage? No, in that time I also had an appendix operation, and after the operation I worked as a bartender for three months. Then I went back.

Last time we asked you in how many languages you could say 'I love you'. You answered that you could not say it in many languages because you never use it. And then you told us about your boyfriend who lives in Bulgaria. You have, as we understand it, a double life. You talk about your love and how you separate it. Is it always easy to make the separation between when you are with your boyfriend and when you are working? It's a big difference.

Can you describe the difference? When I am in Bulgaria for holidays, the first day I don't think about anything, I feel very good. When I am here I'm thinking about money all the time, about holidays in Bulgaria, how fast the day will pass, and when I can go to sleep after that.

Does it ever happen that when you are with your boyfriend you have the same feelings as with your clients? No, never! Me and my boyfriend talk about other things, we don't talk about work and I know that he is my boyfriend. This work is like being a waitress.

You said before that you prefer German clients. Can you explain that? Fast money, you don't have to work a lot.

Can you be more explicit? If you compare: Germans are Germans, there are no others like the Germans. They do whatever you tell them to do. They are robots. To a regular German client I can say that I am not in the mood, that I don't want to make love with him, and he just says nothing and pays.

Why do you think they are like that? I know how they are.

But why? I had a girlfriend when I was in Russia and she told me that Russians are as stupid as Germans. During the war between Russia and Germany the intelligent people were killed and both nations completely degenerated. And it continued in the next generations.

Have you met girls who have just become prostitutes? Have you ever helped them? I have never told other girls to start working, but when I see the Bulgarian girls here in the Czech Republic, I want to help them. Like the Bulgarian girl living downstairs in this hotel, she had a problem because somebody wanted to sell her. The boss doesn't buy and sell girls, but I told him that we could buy her. I loaned her the money. But this girl had to work and give it back to me. Then she could do anything she wanted. I say to the girls that this work isn't good and once they start to earn money, they'll never stop working.

So you and your boss bought the girl downstairs together? I paid for her and I loaned her money. I can't buy the girls and then say to them, 'Bye, go home!'. When a girl pays me back, she can go home or stay here, she can do anything she wants. I need my money back, I don't have money for everybody.

How much money? Not so much. I know how difficult it is abroad. A Bulgarian girl abroad must have a pimp. Otherwise she is very lonely. But when she is here, in this place, she is better off. I know, I've experienced bad times abroad before. It is not much money, but it is my money, that I've earned.

How long a time did it take for that girl to pay her debt? She paid quickly, in three days. After that she had to decide if she wanted to go home or continue to work. This girl wanted to earn some money and went back home last Friday. Every Friday there is a bus between Germany and Bulgaria and there is a bus stop here.

But that girl, she just arrived, didn't she? She was taken here by a pimp, and then she was sold by some Bulgarians. My boss doesn't normally buy and sell girls but he wanted his money back. Then he paid the Bulgarians. It was not much money, but he said it was money from his own pocket. Everybody knows that he does not sell girls.

When you and your girlfriend decided to go to Germany, just before that, what made you go there? We had no visa for Germany, so we decided to go without a visa. I thought that if the police caught us nothing would happen to us, maybe they would just send us back to Bulgaria, that's all.

What happened after, did you walk over, or…? We went from here to Cínovec to the border and tried to sneak in through customs, but we were caught.

Was it the police who caught you? It was the Czech police.

And then, what did they say to you? They locked us up and asked if we had any money, but this Petko bribed the policemen to send any Bulgarian girls that they caught to him. So they were corrupt. And he told the municipal police not to make any problems about the girls.

Did he come to get you out of jail? The police just took us in the car and drove us directly to Petko's bar.

What did he tell you? He wanted to take our passports. They told me in Bulgaria that the passport is a very important document and that I should never give it to anybody, otherwise I'm finished. But there was a boy with us who had our passports and the other papers in his bag, but Petko scared him with a gun and then he had to give it all to him. Then Petko told us to go to the car. We refused. He said if we didn't, we would end up in a box. Then he took us to a flat where he stayed.

This guy Petko, he must have been really happy that he got you, because you are so exceptionally beautiful. Do you feel that you have a value? Do you get any comments? What? I don't understand. When they drove me away, Petko said that he didn't pay anything to the policeman but I don't trust him. But he was happy that I was there to make him some money.

I mean did Petko like some girls more than others? Pretty girls were in one flat and the other girls in the other flat. The pretty girls worked during the day and the others worked during the night. That's the way it was, you always had to do what he wanted.

And where were you? I was working during the day.

Did he demand to sleep with you immediately? No, it was more than a month later.

How did he approach you? He came to me and said, 'Come!'. And I had to go and do whatever he wanted.

So how did you do it with him? The other girls told me that I must do everything wrong, because if I did it well he would want to do it everyday.

How did you feel about your situation? You had been free before, if I understand it right? When I got there I thought, 'Now I can't keep my own wallet, I will be without my own money'. I was very frightened and nervous, psychologically it's very difficult. I think I'm strong. Otherwise I would have gone crazy. It's not only about Petko, even the clients … I'm laughing, but in my heart I'm nervous and scared. I was also afraid that I would be locked up, and many other things also scared me. The girls told me a lot: if you don't have a strong psyche – this is the end.

Did you plan a way to get out of it? I was thinking a lot about how to run away, but at the same time I realized that the policemen would bring me back. It's no problem to run away, but I had no passport. I would have had to go to the police to get new papers: lie and say that my passport had been stolen. I was afraid that the police would just bring me back. I didn't know how things worked in the Czech Republic. I thought that when they caught me on the border, they would send me back to Bulgaria.

There was a rumour about this pimp, what he had done to other girls? There were rumours that he killed a girl. Therefore everybody was scared and silent. When I understood that he had killed a girl, I immediately dropped the idea of running away. I didn't want to die!

Were there any signs that he had problems with the police? He travelled to Tunisia, then the police from Prague were here in a microbus with dark windows and helicopters were flying over his bar. A girl who was working in his bar told me that he was being searched for by the police, and she thought that the police would come within two weeks.

Was there someone else there to run the business for him? He had thirty Bulgarians as bodyguards.

What was your relationship to the bodyguards like? Nothing. We worked, they worked too. It was forbidden to have a relationship with them, he would have killed us.

You more or less lived together in the same house. Did you have any affairs? It was not possible to even think about it. It wasn't worth risking your life for one fuck.

Did he come back, to pick up some more girls? He didn't come back, he sent the bodyguards.

How did he select the girls? He told the bodyguards which girls he wanted to have. And then they bought the tickets.

Did you know where you were going? No. But when I was on the plane I knew.

Did the bodyguards tell you where you were going? They said, 'Let's go for a holiday'. We didn't trust them but we had to go.

How was it to arrive in Tunisia? We lived in a hotel, we went to the beach everyday. We ate and slept a lot. I think he planned to start a business there, with girls. But I'm not sure.

What happened in Tunisia? Was there a warrant on him? Interpol was searching for him. And he was thinking of where to go. A place where Interpol doesn't work. He was thinking of Cuba, and then about a country where there was a war, but he was afraid that it would be difficult to bring the girls. I don't remember what country it was. He was also thinking about passing through the desert, a safari in a Jeep. Finally, we went to Russia. He wanted to start a business there too, but it was impossible because the Russian Mafia is much stronger than him. He was very small by then. Then we went to Vladivostok and later to Korea.

Did he talk to you girls about the problems he had? Later he was talking, but not much. He was very scared and became very small, and he was lying to us.

What was he lying about? He told us that we would not have to work, but to the bodyguards he said that we girls would be working, but without getting paid. He and his bodyguards would share the money. In the end he lied to the bodyguards too. He didn't give them any money, not even for food. So they stole all the passports and money and we escaped.

Let us just finish the story about Korea. They stole all the passports and the money from him. We lived in different hotels. And they gave us some of the money and our passports. They told us, 'Now you can do whatever you want'.

So after that you came back here? Yes, I needed more money, so I came back here, and, when I have enough money, I will go home to Bulgaria.

Honza

Motel Hubert, Dubi, 24/07/99

ANN-SOFI How long have you been in this motel and how did you get the idea for it? **HONZA** I started here six years ago with the street walking business and I had a money exchange office. I was renting the place and I liked it, next door another space was available and I rented that one too, and made a motel out of it. Just accommodation without any bar service. One year later I made a bar in there, so one of the rooms got smaller.

Did you have girls in the motel? Was that the business idea? It was only a motel and the girls just came here. I never had my own girls. The girls came from the street. There weren't as many motels as there are today. Six years ago it was a third of what it is today. So the possibility was here, and I said, 'it's a business'. And that's how I started out.

Was it different on the street then? Almost the same, but there were more girls standing outside, but now with more motels, the girls are inside or in front of the motel. Back then they were standing everywhere.

Tell us something about yourself, before you had the motel, when you were young. I went to restaurant school and I became a waiter. I started out in restaurants as a manager and waiter for about thirty years. That was during Communism.

Here? No, no. I was in Krkonose. Krkonose, Jablonec, and later in Teplice. In 1979, I ran the Hotel Sport here in Dubi. You know, the one that closed up. Now it's a ruin. He inherited it – Lobkowitz – after the restitution. So in '79 the prostitution was already there, but it ran only through the trucks. No passenger cars stopped back then. The prostitution already existed then. It was already happening. The Communists knew about it, but it was covered up, as if nothing was going on. So the prostitution has really been here for the past twenty years.

Have you had any rough times or problems since you've had the motel? And who is out there, Russians or Ukrainians? More gangs from Teplice … gypsies.

How did you deal with that? Well, at first they came and wanted to borrow money. Since I had money I lent it to them, a small amount, only 1000 Korunas. So when they showed up the next time they said they were sorry, they couldn't pay me back. I told them that if they asked for money again it would be blackmail, and I would defend myself in a certain way. So they didn't come back anymore.

So you don't need anybody for protection? A bouncer would only attract other guys, troublemakers, and then we'd have a problem. With just a woman [Katja] around, they don't dare to bother.

Are there Russians around? Do they cause any problems? Russians make problems. They make problems for anyone who has Russian or Polish women. I was scared to hire any Russian women because I knew their guys would ask for money, or take the girls away. That Yugoslavian guy up there had problems with that. The Russians came, but he's backed by the Yugoslavian Mafia. So he called for them. They had already beaten up the Russian guys twice. So the Russians took off.

So the Russians think that the Russian women belong to them? Yes, they think that they belong to them. If I had Russian girls here, that would definitely be a problem. Also, none of the girls here belong to me. I have an agreement with them for accommodation. They pay me for that and for food, but I get no money from the prostitution.

How do the girls get to the motel? Do they come alone, or is someone with them? They come alone. The Bulgarian Mafia was here with girls. All the guys got locked up, but one girl [Vanja] who worked for them stayed, as she had to be in court as a witness. She had no place to stay so she rented a room here. She wasn't allowed to leave the country until the lawsuit was over. In the meantime, the Hungarian girl [Andrea] came. They got to know each other. She stayed for three months and then went home. She was gone for a year, and now she's back again.

We have heard about this pimp, this Petko guy… Petko rented

half of this motel. I had the police here; they were looking for him. But he had already left; he bought a villa up here in Dubi. So all of them moved out, his whole gang. He knew he would mess up my business; that's why he ran away. We had agreed on that.

Half of your property? Yes, half of it. The Red Bar under construction.

How was it to rent the house to Petko? He pretended to be a big shot. He changed cars a lot and he wore a hat. He showed off that he was a Mafia guy. And his mother – he had his mother here – they called her 'Mama'! And she kind of watched out for the whole gang. But all of them got locked up. There were so many of them! About fifty girls. They had to work on shifts, and they had to give all the money away. Here in Dubi he built himself some sort of glass box. He exhibited the girls there. He had two glass boxes here, and opened another one in Chomutov. He also had two glass boxes in Semic.

Glass boxes? Separate from the house? Why did he do that? The girls could be seen there, in the boxes. There was a roof, and, underneath, a bed. Dirt on everything. And the Germans went there. I wouldn't even clean my shoes there. Those Germans are into things I don't understand. And I don't care. In the end they locked a girl up in the basement, and she got a cold. They forgot about her, and she died in that basement. They buried her. When Petko ran away, a Bulgarian guy filed a complaint that a girl was buried. So the cops looked for her with a helicopter. And they found her. Nobody from that gang knows exactly who murdered the girl. They don't know. But Vanja saw scenes from the courthouse on TV. When they led the guys to court, she pointed and said, 'That's him!'. But she can't tell anybody because then they would come after her.

So Vanja was there then? In that place? Yes, of course.

Did she also work in the glass boxes? Yes!

Do the girls get along with each other? Do they fight? Is there competition? Yes, they fight. The tall, blond one works for those pimps, the gypsies. Gotta make sure they don't hear that ... the gypsies. If she doesn't bring them money they are nasty to her ... they don't give her food. She has problems with them. So she really has to go for it. She has to make her money. The other girls don't have to; they're not under such pressure. If a girl is better looking and the others are rude to her, then she fights back. There are fights, but they don't get physical.

What do the girls do with their free time? Well, here, our girls sleep, but I hear the blond girl has to work. She helps with the groceries, and helps clean up their home. I just don't understand her, I don't know why she does that, she has a kid in Jablonec and her parents live there too. She practically does it for free. The gypsies promised to put money into her savings account. But that isn't true. She doesn't get anything!

How does it make you feel to know that? A couple of years ago I felt sorry for her, the gypsies behaved much worse then. They made the girls stand outside in short pants when it was snowing. The gypsies sat inside the bar and screamed at the girls. When they asked for hot tea, they would say, 'Not until you bring us some money.' They would scream things like, 'Your ass is fat!'. Rain or snow, they had to stay outside in their short pants! These days it's not like that anymore. I mean, now only the gypsies do that. The white guys don't do that. A girl works for a white guy, it doesn't get that far. But with a gypsy it does.

What do you think of the mentality of the gypsies? How do they think? Well, gypsies, they have a bad character. You can't be friends with gypsies. They are false. I mean, dishonest. It doesn't make sense to build up any kind of friendship. It's totally senseless. The superficial friendship, like, 'Hello, how are you?', is OK, but you can't do business with them. Any business with them is bad. They are people with a different mentality. But the gypsies are more sociable than other people. They stick together and meet more often than normal people. They help each other. If someone is locked up they send packages.

Are you afraid of anything? Well, nowadays, if you're in the business you are afraid. Because in our country the laws are bad. Today, if a girl reports you and says that you are holding her against her will, or if two girls agree, I mean without reason, and claim that I lock them up, then they sentence you. In our country they don't investigate that. You automatically go to jail. People get locked up for two years without any reason while the girls keep working for somebody else. There are lots of innocent people locked up. I know a lot of them who are in jail for two years without reason. The girl doesn't even have to go for questioning anymore. And the guys are still locked up. The girls do it on purpose. And sometimes the cops help them. We had a case here, a lady with two girls, one from Prague, pretty girls. Some pimps were here, and liked one of these two girls. The pimps called the police, asked them to bring the girls in for questioning. The girl that wasn't so pretty they let go, but gave the other one to the pimps. The pimps paid the police 500 Deutschmarks and took the girl away.

Do you think the police are corrupt here? They are corrupt! The cops take bribes from the foreigners because they're not afraid of them. But they'd never take a bribe from me. Once, I wanted to have a certain thing completed. The region of Usti nad Labem was handling this. So I went to a Yugoslavian guy, I gave him some money and he brought me all the papers I needed. If I went there myself they'd accuse me of bribery. They take bribes from the Vietnamese, Russians, Yugoslavians. They're not afraid of foreigners. That's why they all have work permits. For example, sixty Vietnamese are registered in one apartment. The police don't do anything about it because they've taken bribes.

Can you tell us something about your personal life? How you met Katja, and so on? How I met Katja? I know her father very well, we are the same age. We used to work together in Usti nad Labem as waiters. We were the best of all the waiters. So we had to serve the Communists. We served the Chairman of the Communist Party, of the Central Bohemian Region; we also served the other parties from the region. We had keys to the government villa and we went there with scholars, and we worked together there. That's how I got to know her father. Later,

I had the exchange office up the road. The girl lived kind of a wild life, so her father asked me to take care of her; he asked me if she could help me, that she would like that. She had a grammar school education. I agreed to take her and after three weeks we fell in love with each other. Ever since then we've been together.

The clients that come here, do you speak to them? What kind of people are they? It's bad now. But five years ago we had the rich West Germans. Now it's mostly East Germans. Before we had clients from everywhere. It was better before. Now we have a lot of young ones coming, but they go to disco clubs. It's simply not the same anymore.

Do you also have steady clients? It changes ... it depends on the girl. If the girl stays half a year, she has her steady clients. But if the girls change often, then it's bad. They are looking for clients, and there aren't many new clients anymore. So it's better if a girl stays here for, say, a year. Then she has maybe four or five steady clients. She just arranges everything on the phone. A year ago I had five pretty girls. Not mine. A pimp had them. I told you about it. A friend came from Teplice with a Spanish guy. He asked them to go to Spain for a month. They never came back. Those girls had four to five steady clients each. Everything arranged by phone.

Have you had problems with the clients? Germans? Yes, they get drunk and they get noisy...

Have you had to interfere? No, mostly not. They don't usually dare to say anything against the women. When Katja raises her voice, they get quiet. She hasn't had any real problems with them. They are pigs sometimes without any culture. That's true. Katja is very tactical. Once, a Russian guy came here from Prague in a taxi. Big shot, big body. Rich guy. He broke glasses, touched the girls, while the taxi driver waited outside. He gave Katja 1000 marks for his drinks. He was destroying the business. I wanted to go after him, but Katja said, 'Please don't go, you're gonna fight.' And she was trying to reach somebody on the cellphone. Katja solved the situation very tactfully. She said to the taxi driver, 'You saw him giving me 1000 marks, right?.' He said yes, so she gave him 300 marks to take the Russian away. An hour later he was gone. They drove off somewhere.

Do you think that sometimes the men who come here are shy? They are sometimes.

Does it help to talk to them? To make them feel at ease? Sure, I offer them alcohol. Or recommend the girl that is good.

Do they tell you things about their lives? They don't talk to me that much. But they talk to Katja; yes they do. About the problems they have and so on.

What do you see in the future for yourself and the motel? It will get worse. With every year it gets worse and worse. It doesn't look good for the future. That's why I decided to organize some trips for Germans to the Czech Republic. Live Czech music and food. They can dance and have fun. So I see things moving more in that direction in the future.

Do you think it will work without the girls too? As long as this is the main route to Germany, the girls will be here. But they are preparing a new highway to Dresden.

Do you have any children with her [Katja]? No, I don't. But there is an age difference between us. Katja would like one but I'm still thinking about it. So, I'm still not sure. I'm thinking about it. I'm still young!

How do you think this scene influences a child? The TV influences children more than what's here. If you turn NOVA on, they repeat movies from the night before, and the children are exposed to sex and aggression. So I think it's worse for the kids than what is happening here. But, besides that, we don't live here anyway.

Is there something you really want to do in your life? I would love to have more leisure time. Spend more time with Katja. In Novy Bor I have a nice country-house with a tennis court. I haven't been there for over half a year, so we are not using it. Some other people live in it now. In the future I want to hire some good friends to run the motel for us. Another solution would be a good sale to someone who can take over the whole business, or to rent it to some reliable people. My brother has two businesses here. Some people pay him and he has no problems with it. It's common to pay 70,000 to 100,000 Korunas per month to rent a business like this.

Regarding my hobbies, I like sports, the tourist kind, like skiing. I used to race in Teplice in 1980. That's a hobby I've had my whole life. We used to go to the Alps in Slovakia, a bunch of guys in a VW-van. The last time we were in Innsbruck and we liked it a lot. We've also been in Angorra and in the Savoy Alps and in Slovakia. I also like another sport, diving. I've been doing it for three years now. I have my licence from Perry. The company has its headquarters in California and their instructors gave courses in Prague. My nephew has a diving school in Teplice now. He rents out equipment and prepares people for diving. They went to Africa and I decided to go with them. I didn't have any experience. We were at the sea the first day and he asked me, 'So Uncle, are you going down with us?'. I said, 'I don't know but I'll tell you when we get back in the evening.' So he had a classroom there and he taught me everything, all the signs, etc. The next morning they dressed me up and we went down holding hands. I liked it so much that I have my own complete equipment now. I went to Africa three times and to Yugoslavia three times. So I'm a diver now! I've also completed an advanced course. So I can go down with people below 40 metres to do wreck and night dives from a boat. Even in America they know that it's really something to have this. You are somebody. And they don't look at you like a jerk anymore. And I have it!

Kvéta

Hostel at Mielnik, near Prague, 04/02/99

ANN-SOFI What is your name and how old are you? **KVÉTA** My
name is Kvéta, I'm twenty-four years old. I come from Rakovnik,
a small town 40 kilometres from Prague. I'm an only child. I lived
there with my mother and stepfather, who raped me. And I have
not had any contact with my family for the last seven years.

Where does your mother work? She works in a car factory.

How was your life before your stepfather moved in? And tell us
about your mother? I'm half Czech, half Slovakian. My real father
was an alcoholic, and he beat us a lot. Later, my mother also
became an alcoholic. They did not take care of me and were
often not at home. I have a feeling I don't know my parents.

When was the first time your stepfather sexually abused you? I
was still in school, and I had just met my first love and I was
happy. I told my mother. My stepfather was there as well and he
became jealous, and told me that he wanted to take my virginity
instead of my boyfriend. So he raped me. When I told my mother
she was angry but did not want to press charges or contact the
police. I told her that when I was eighteen I would move out.

Did it happen when your mother was away? She was at home.

How was that possible? My mother has a problem with her heart.
She goes to bed early, so she was sleeping when he raped me. I
woke up my mother, but she didn't realize what had happened.
The next morning she got angry and promised to kick him out.
But she didn't. To get away from him I locked myself up in the
bathroom, or my own room. But he broke in, and raped me again.
The third time it happened I had enough and left them. But my
mother has continued to live with this man.

How did your stepfather defend himself? First, he ignored it all,
saying I was lying. But my mother didn't trust him. She believed
me! She thought it was impossible to lie about something like
that. Afterwards he came to my room begging on his knees,
asking for forgiveness! I told him I could forgive him a lot of
things but never this. Then I told my mother that this is my life,

and I have the right to decide whom I want to live with, and so I left.

You had a boyfriend, what happened with the relationship? I broke up with him, because I was so full of hate that I couldn't stand him touching me. He didn't understand why. I explained that I might get violent with him.

What happened after you left home? In the beginning I slept at the railway station, or stayed with friends. Then I met a new boyfriend but he died. After that I began drinking. I was very depressed. And I went to Cheb in South Bohemia.

How did he die? He was killed in a motorcycle accident. When I slept in the railway station, living on what people gave me, I soon realized I could not continue like that. Finally, I found a job. And later I started working in a nightclub in Cheb, where I was dancing. After a while my girlfriend suggested that we go to France. She told me about a well-paid job in a bar. But she didn't tell the truth. My girlfriend actually sold me. I met her when I was in difficult situation, I was addicted to drugs. At that time my girlfriend took care of me and helped me quit the drugs. She was forty years old and had a daughter that was just a little bit younger than me. Eventually I even moved in with her family. I helped them clean. When they needed money I gave it to them but at the time I didn't know that her husband was trafficking – selling girls. So when they suggested that I work in France, I didn't know it would be in a bordello. If I had known I would never have accepted it.

And then...? I went to Cheb where I stayed a month while they prepared my departure. I really believed that the job as a bar-tender existed. My girlfriend was making phone calls to France in front of me. When I arrived I was met by another woman who told me I had been sold. I had to give her my passport. My girlfriend went back to the Czech Republic. They took me to a hotel. They gave me a T-shirt and shorts and shoes, and then told me to go working on the street until 7 a.m. the next morning.

What did you say? What was your response? There was not a chance to say a word or to escape. They were in contact with the Turkish Mafia and were very cruel with the girls. It was impossible to say anything, or else you would get beaten. Once I tried to run away, but I was caught by the Turks. They pushed me into the river. After that they beat me and then raped me in a field. So it was better not to say anything. Each girl was controlled by someone.

So what happened the first day? The first day I was on the street, I was completely terrified. I didn't understand French and they didn't speak any German. I was afraid to get into the cars, so when they stopped I just opened the door and slammed it shut again. Some of the other girls noticed that I didn't make any money, so they beat me. My pimp was a Czech woman. She never touched us, but she had Arab or Turkish men who did whatever she demanded – to beat us, to take a girl away and kill her.

Who was this woman? How old was she, and what did she look like? And where did she live? A normal woman, forty-five years old, blond. She lived with us in our room in the hotel. She never went out because the police were waiting outside to arrest all of them. If she wanted something she asked one of the girls to go out and buy it.

Why didn't the police enter the hotel? The hotel staff never let the police in. They phoned the rooms so the pimps and girls could hide. There are laws in France that say that the police need a warrant to make a raid. The police told us that if three girls make a complaint, saying there is a pimp in the hotel, they could close the hotel. Which is what finally happened.

Was it the first time you had worked as a prostitute, when you were in France? Yes.

Do you remember your first client, the first car you entered, and what happened? A client came. I told him the price depending on what he asked for. Then we went to a parking lot. I only worked inside cars, we were not allowed to go to a hotel.

Do you remember any special incident, something beyond the normal? Once I was taken into a BMW by a good-looking client. We were in one of the controlled parking lots and, although there was another girl watching, he began to strangle me, and nobody helped me. I had to try to get out by myself.

What did he say? How did it begin? First he paid. We were only allowed to do it with a rubber. But he didn't want to do it with a rubber. But he finally agreed to use one. But when it was over, he wasn't satisfied and wanted his money back. I didn't want to give him his money back. I told him I had done my work, so there was no reason for him to get it back. From somewhere in the car he took a sock and began to strangle me.

How did you manage to get out of the car? The car didn't have an automatic lock system, and at this moment I became so strong that I broke out of his hands and out of the car.

What happened then, did you go back to the hotel? I had to get back to working on the street.

What did you do at the hotel when you were not working? Was there anything else you did, or were you always inside your room? Did you have any fun … talking to the other girls, etc.? We had no chance to have fun or to talk because we were at the hotel with the pimp woman all the time. She slept in our room.

How many girls in one room? We were five to six girls in a room.

Do you remember the other girls? There was a sixteen-year-old girl who was stolen and sold many times. A very close friend of mine was finally killed by the woman pimp in a bus station. We had no chance to talk to each other on the street. We only exchanged a few words with the clients.

The pimp woman was not on the street, and you still felt you could not talk to each other? We were under total control. When we got back at eight o'clock in the morning, she already knew about everything: how many clients we had had, how much money we had made, if we had used a rubber or not. She knew everything.

You said earlier that you had been forced under water. What had happened just before? I was with a client and just before his orgasm he started to beat me, to kick me in the head, I was bleeding. I think he did this to increase his own pleasure. I got so pissed off, I ran away and hid myself in another hotel. But two Turkish guys found me. There was a river nearby. They took my head and forced my face under the water.

What happened then? I went back to the hotel. I got dressed up and went back to the street … I had a date with one of my steady clients who liked me. I asked him to take care of me, and he helped me to escape to another hotel. A week later the Turkish guys found me again. They drove me back again. For a few days nothing happened. One evening a French client, a young boy, took me in his car to a cornfield where there were already four cars parked and a lot of Turkish men waiting. They all anally raped me. They stole all my personal belongings, my money, my papers, etc. They also had a strong paralyzing spray. It's a German spray; you're blind for half an hour. They sprayed me in my face and anus. Yes, anywhere it was possible. Then they drove away. I had to walk back to the hotel.

Can you describe the pimp woman? This pimp woman used to live with a Turkish man in France. She began trafficking – buying and selling women – six years ago. Once they tied me up to a tree in the forest and beat me with a stick. The pimp woman was laughing all the time and asking me if I was going to continue to try to escape, threatening that if I tried again, she was ready to kill me. I told her I would never try to run away again. After this she took me out to a restaurant. We had dinner together and later I went back to the hotel, washed myself, took a shower and went back to work on the street.

For how long were you in France? Three months.

Please explain how your client finally helped you to get out of

France? I stayed for three days in my client's house. After that I lived in an asylum house. There were a lot of people there, families with children. We slept on the floor; we had to leave the building at five in the morning and could return only at seven in the evening. My problem was that I didn't have any papers to leave the country. After a while my client found the 'La Strada' organization in France. They contacted the same organization in Prague. And they finally organized my papers and paid for my ticket to come back here.

You said that eventually there was a raid in the hotel. Did that happen when you were still there? I was not there any longer, but I heard that the police closed some of the hotels, arrested a few pimps whom they deported to the Czech Republic.

So they are here now? Yes.

Warte Mal!
Installed at Musée d'art Moderne de la Ville de Paris, 2001

The other girls told me that I must do
everything wrong,

ht, Radek drove Katja to a bar late at
pick up the car from Honza who was
nk to drive. It was Honza who suggested
on the phone that Radek should drive
n. When they arrived, Honza asked her
y why she didn't just leave with Radek.
Honza shows up at the bar and asks
o help him prepare the grill in the
d.

oks hungover and emotionally drained;
x-communist waiter.

own from my room at noon. Kveta had

Warte Mal!
(Hey Wait!)
Robert Fleck

Visitors find themselves face to face with a whole town. The architecture is physical, imaginary and virtual: screens with images of conversations, filmed portraits and private moments. Ann-Sofi Sidén has arranged and installed various immaterial experiences and images in such a way that visitors feel themselves transported into a 'real-life' situation that consists solely of video, which in turn gives it a particularly abstract quality: in effect a visual metaphor that fills the entire space, albeit with images and sound-tracks that appear to be documentary in character.

The virtual town in the installation *Warte Mal!* does not, however, rely primarily on theoretical principles as do many other works that borrow the devices of architecture, film, sculpture, performance and documentary. On the contrary, the rigorous aesthetic of Sidén's installation concentrates on the many and varied components of human existence in an urban and rural context: individual life stories with intense heights, depths, hopes, expectation and disintegration – all at once. *Warte Mal!* draws its strength from the fact that the feelings and passions that go to make up a town and its life are its main focus: people of all kinds, with diverse social functions and conflicting positions living out different social roles, their characters – appealing, unappealing, moving, heroic or unremarkable – fashioned by their various positions and the degree of power they exert.

At first sight, life in the Czech town of Dubi, where most of the films were shot, seems quite normal, even comfortable. Sidén's documentary sequences show beautiful summer days and cold, but equally beautiful, winter days. People in Dubi seem to live like people anywhere. But one particular feature, the mainstay of the 'local economy', turns the situation into an elaborate metaphor for human and geo-political processes today. For Dubi is a centre for the mass prostitution that has been operating for over ten years along the borders between the former Communist states and Western Europe. These films from the Czech Republic – with their calm, consciously slow-moving and seemingly idyllic aspect – portray a human catastrophe of immense proportions, an outrage in the heart of Europe, a symbol of the extreme tensions that are rife at the beginning of the twenty-first century. It is to Sidén's credit, and no mean achievement, that she has found an artistic form for such dramatic moments and macro-political processes, creating an intense, audio-visual sculpture that addresses human suffering yet avoids narrative illustration and moral censure. In this respect, *Warte Mal!* reflects our own epoch. With the simplest of means, this large-scale installation shows that the relatively new medium of video installation has come of age and has secured its place in the history of sculpture.

Dubi is a desolate town in the Czech mountains, six kilometres from the German border. It lies on the E55, a two-lane road that has been increasingly used as a transit route between the East and the West since 1989. Until the demise of Communism in autumn 1989, also known as 'The Velvet Revolution', Dubi was behind the Iron Curtain, that closely-guarded border which no citizen from the Eastern Bloc could cross to enter the West. In those days, each and every person would be stopped by Czech and Russian soldiers. The border that had been there for centuries was closed. In late 1989 it was opened again. And ever since then, day and night, as heavily-laden trucks thunder through, the road has been lined on both sides by hundreds of young girls and women from all over Eastern Europe. They are working as prostitutes, selling their bodies to the truck drivers and any other men passing through. There is such fierce competition between them that, at times, they take extreme risks as they step out into the traffic, crying *Warte Mal!* (Hey Wait!) to make any German drivers stop. These are often the first words of German that they speak, as we learn from Sidén's work.

The soliciting that goes on at the western border of the Czech Republic, and other borders up and down the eastern edge of the European Union, is a phenomenon that leaves a deep, lasting impression on all those who witness it. The relentless mass exploitation of young girls and women fills anyone who sees it with the sense of having arrived at a geo-political fault line. Clearly lodged in my own mind is a moment in July 1993 when two young Austrian artists told me in horror, at times lost for words, of what they had seen along this road. Four years later, in May 1997, I saw it for myself, unexpectedly, on my first trip during the preparations for the European biennial *Manifesta 2*, with curators Maria Lind and Barbara Vanderlinden. We were so shocked that, months later, we still felt the need to tell others about what we had witnessed.

For a visual artist, such extreme situations, phenomena and issues are *a priori* impossible topics for a work of art. It all seems too emotive and at the same time too heavily loaded with journalistic and literary clichés: there is no room for anything other than a moral response. Having been an eye-witness, I could never have imagined that an artist would manage to enter into and speak about this situation straightforwardly and persuasively, deriving material from it for a large-scale audio-visual installation such as *Warte Mal!*, which has an open, fluent touch and yet is convincing as a three-dimensional piece, and never moralizes. Sidén has found a way to create a precise work from this scandal, one that above all gives the viewer an intense insight into certain internal processes of the human psyche.

Warte Mal! is shaped by three main features. Firstly, by using a spatial montage, the artist has skilfully exploited the diversity and complexity of a small town like Dubi. The virtual town is made up of films and pictures of all different kinds. There is Honza, the owner of the hotel, and Katja, his wife, supporters of the Communist regime that collapsed in November 1989. There are the policemen and a number of other small-time local bosses. And then there are the clients – men passing through from Western Europe – and the prostitutes from all over Central and Eastern Europe. The result is an extremely international community in which Czechs are the minority. Sidén's work presents an extraordinary 'internal report' on this self-contained world. Even on a cursory viewing of the work, one cannot help learning from the sound-track that, in our own day and age, criminals in Central and Eastern Europe make concerted raids on discos and other places where they kidnap young girls aged between fifteen and eighteen and force them to work as prostitutes. In *Warte Mal!*, the artist shows yet another dimension of this situation, namely the circumstances of those living in the Czech Republic whose skin colour and ethnic background mark them out as Romanies. In Dubi, as in the rest of the Czech Republic, they are treated by everyone else as second-class citizens. Some of the Romanies have prostitutes working along the road, others are seen from time to time selling clothes, make-up and other items to the girls working in the bars. According to the scale of values that most people in Dubi seem to share, the Romanies are right at the bottom. *Warte Mal!* is a world in its own right that one is caught up in as soon as one sets step in it.

The work itself was prompted by an art project, 'Midnight Walkers & City Sleepers', that took place in the red-light district of Amsterdam in 1999. Sidén turned her attention away from Amsterdam and conducted her research in the Czech Republic instead. After exhibiting the work in Amsterdam, Sidén continued to visit the people she had met in the Czech Republic, and formed *Warte Mal!*. This was first shown as a complete work at the artist's solo exhibition at the Wiener Secession, where it consisted of individual portraits and themed observations ('Dubi Morning', 'Party Room', 'Diary', 'Road Projections'). Different types of film, dialogue with the text within the images, shown on monitors in glazed booths, and diverse scenery sequences, as well as scrolling diary text, generate a varied rhythm that lead from one large-scale projection to another. This rhythm of different pictorial forms served as an anchor for the ensemble as in a larger-than-life 'multiptych'. The sure touch of this discontinuous montage gave one the clear sense that Sidén had been working for some considerable time with feature film forms, bringing together performance, experimental sculpture and a striving for art focused on content and internal mental processes. Since the outset of her career over ten years ago, video has been one of the artist's preferred forms of expression. Her experience making films such as *The Clock Tower* (1995) and *QM, I think I call her QM* (with Tony Gerber, 1997) makes itself felt in the formal structures of *Warte Mal!* despite its very different architectural principles.

The second formal aspect of *Warte Mal!* derives from the fact that the aesthetic of the video tapes is extremely simple and modest. Sidén lived with the people she filmed on various occasions over a period of nine months. Such natural, easy conversations would otherwise scarcely have been possible. The uncomplicated, direct approach that she takes is inventive and skilled. Her video images seem at first sight amateurish, but they are in fact filmed and edited with great precision and very consciously adopt the casual style of holiday videos. With her outwardly naïve, amateur touch, Sidén sets herself apart from the dominant trend in video installations of recent years, with their special effects and extreme illusionism requiring feature film sized budgets – unwittingly moving ever closer to the neo-historical painting of the nineteenth century. In comparison to these, *Warte Mal!* is a welcome indication that it is also possible to work with very simple means entirely in one's own control, as long as, that is, one has an independent aesthetic and a painterly approach.

The interviews shot with a digital hand-held camera also allow the artist to engage intensely and openly with other people's minds and spirits. This is the main impulse behind Sidén's work, and the third and final principle underpinning *Warte Mal!*. The hand-held camera lets the exhibition visitor see the artist's interlocutors through her own eyes. The result is a sequence of very private, intimate situations where empathy for the 'other' comes markedly to the fore. And the engagement with the mentality of the 'other' subverts any moralizing attitudes, since each person is accepted as an individual in his or her own right.

In view of this, it makes sense to draw a comparison here with the installation *Days Inn* . . . of 1998, a piece that Ann-Sofi Sidén made for the exhibition *Nuit Blanche* at the Musée d'art Moderne de la Ville de Paris; she later expanded the idea and produced a new work, *Who Told The Chambermaid?*, for *Manifesta 2* in Luxemburg; following this it was shown as an autonomous piece in the main exhibition of the Venice Biennale in 1999. *Who Told The Chambermaid?* consists of a shelf imitating those in a hotel store room. In between sheets, towels and other paraphernalia are numerous security monitors that show black-and-white video pictures of anonymous yet real private and workplace situations from a hotel; the visitor cannot tell whether these are live pictures or video recordings, or even whether they show acted out sequences or the activities of people unaware that they are under observation.

Two features from *Who Told The Chambermaid?* reappear in

Warte Mal!, although on a larger scale. Firstly, the spatial montage and juxtaposition of monitors and projection surfaces in the work recall the 'all-over' of American Abstract Expressionism, above all rhythm and the negation of perspective by the striking two-dimensionality of the canvas or of the monitor. The particular strength of both works derives from the fact that right from the outset Ann-Sofi Sidén conceived and thought of the video installations in spatial terms. Video is used as a constitutive element in the design of the space, thereby circumventing the clichés of television.

Moreover, in both *Warte Mal!* and *Who Told The Chambermaid?*, the reality status of the moving images is very much up in the air. The images could so easily be fiction, all the more so in view of the fact that Ann-Sofi Sidén had consciously and openly included fictional moments in *Who Told The Chambermaid?*. Three-quarters of this installation is semi-arranged fictional scenes in the hotel rooms. Although *Warte Mal!* consists of purely documentary material, the unidentified reality status of the films also plays an important role in this work. At the first showing of *Warte Mal!* in the Wiener Secession, more than a few people reproached the artist for having presented a 'fiction', unable to believe that things could in fact be 'that bad'. Yet this footage was shot a mere three hours' car drive away from Vienna and, less than an hour's drive from Vienna, precisely the same scenes are being played out on Austria's borders with Slovakia and Hungary.

In further respects *Who Told The Chambermaid?* and *Warte Mal!* can again be seen as two sides of the same coin. In both works, Ann-Sofi Sidén tried out three different modes of realization and presentation before she felt that the work was finished. The two pieces with surveillance monitors, *Days Inn . . .* and *Who Told The Chambermaid?*, were shown in very different forms in Paris, Luxemburg and Venice. In the case of *Warte Mal!*, it is similarly important for the artist that the work has gone through different stages: the first part was shown in Amsterdam's red-light district as a three-channel TV monitor piece, displayed in a café window. In Vienna, it was shown as an in-situ piece, developed specifically for an architectural space and for the geo-political context that affects any exhibition

venue in Central Europe today; following this, *Warte Mal!*
featured as one of the three works – each filling an entire room –
that made up Sidén's partial retrospective in the Musée d'art
Moderne de la Ville de Paris. In the Hayward Gallery, the
presentation of *Warte Mal!* establishes the ensemble of thirteen
videos as an autonomous sculpture, no longer open to alteration,
in the same way that Sidén has made no further changes to *Who
Told The Chambermaid?* since the Venice Biennale in 1999. In its
London setting, *Warte Mal!* takes on some new aspects. In
Vienna, the work abruptly confronted the public with a
suppressed reality of their own region and lives. (Since the end of
Communism, young prostitutes from Eastern Europe, kidnapped
and exploited by the same Mafia networks, can be seen on the
outskirts of many European cities.) The focus in the Viennese
context was on the opposites 'intolerance/tolerance', on the
conflicts and the contradictions between life in the West and in
the East. In Paris, *Warte Mal!* had a particular significance in the
history of the form itself, as a response by a Scandinavian artist
with experience in America to the 1990s generation of French
artists who were very much appropriating and questioning the
cinema aesthetics of *nouvelle vague* and its successors. Now, in
London, *Warte Mal!* finds itself in a multi-cultural context that
again gives the work an added meaning. The Czech border town
it centres on is a collecting place for people from a diversity of
cultures and lands, all trying to come to terms with barely
visible, yet tangible, geo-political processes on a scale that few
can deal with. One need only imagine this work being shown in
London to realize the importance of the multi-cultural context to
Warte Mal! The work portrays people from very different places
in an intellectual environment that is concerned with
reconstructing national identities. The tension communicated in
this work must make it one of the most important works of art on
the subject of multi-culturalism today.

Finally, in one practical matter, *Who Told The Chambermaid?*
is also clearly a forerunner of *Warte Mal!*. For the large-scale
presentation of the former in Luxemburg, Sidén had to shoot the
films in a hotel. She chose a hotel where she had stayed on
earlier visits to see the exhibition space. In order to secure
permission to shoot the film from each individual member of staff

in the hotel, she lived with them for some time. Her aim was to win over the staff and guests, and the additional typecast 'actors', to the idea of an artist being in the hotel and of her freely creating a work in this 'world in miniature'. The fact of artist and protagonists living in close proximity also changed the work. The situation in *Warte Mal!* was very similar. Sidén's long stays in Dubí – in the very hotel where she finally shot most of the films – allowed the various individuals to be so open to her as an artist. This was also the source of the immense trust that gives the content of this work its strength. There is, however, one major difference compared to *Who Told The Chambermaid?*. In the earlier work, Sidén filmed the hotel staff and guests pursuing their daily business, anonymously carrying out tasks. In order to do this freely, to be able to film her subjects without attracting attention to herself and without her subjects becoming involved, she had to prepare and talk individually to each one. *Warte Mal!* reverses this situation: the conversations with different individuals become the material of the installation. While there is direct, carefully planned communication between the artist and the people in the hotel in *Who Told The Chambermaid?*, the later large-format sculpture concentrates on uncovering the internal process, which then becomes the main content of the work. Additionally, one aspect that radically differentiates the two works is that *Who Told The Chambermaid?* has no sound at all, whereas *Warte Mal!* is built on both images and individual voices as well as ambient sound.

Ann-Sofi Sidén began her career in a region mid-way between performances (using her own body, objects, images and sculptural aspects) and documentary film. She exemplifies a generation of artists who were still affected in the early 1980s by the performative and 'anti-form' discourse of the 1970s avant-garde. These artists were somewhat marginalized by the spec-tacular art forms of the 1980s. In the early 1990s, this seemingly 'lost generation' took on central importance due to the continuity of their engagement with anti-form, political, feminist and concept or body art themes. But Sidén refused the mainstream of political correctness in art, preferring somewhat awkward forms that were virtually incomprehensible at that time, such as the fictional 35mm film. When the documentary paradigm started to dominate the art of the younger generation in the mid-to-late 1990s through the influence of Nan Goldin, Sidén was somewhere else, producing emotionally-charged installations such as *Who Has Enlarged This Hole?* (1994), *It is by confining one's neighbour that one is convinced of one's own sanity* (1995) and, as a result of these two works, the film *QM, I think I call her QM* (1997); she was also already involved in the preliminary stages of spatial installations using filmed material to address the psyche and states of mind, as in *Who Told The Chambermaid?* and *Warte Mal!*. With these works, Ann-Sofi Sidén has become a key figure in contemporary art.

Warte Mal! is primarily a large-scale fresco or multiptych portraying a multi-cultural community: a community that collects together all the contradictions of the macro- and micro-political situations on the European continent, like a mixture in a test tube. In this respect, it is like an *allégorie réelle*, in the sense that Baudelaire used the term for similar works in the mid-nineteenth century. The work focuses on the passions that are central to our own time: success, the thirst for profit and Western living standards, national pride combined with a readiness to use force and to subjugate others for the sake of the dream of a normal, *petit-bourgeois* existence. In this respect, *Warte Mal!* is probably the most complex, realistic and open-minded work about the situation in Central and Eastern Europe since the collapse of Communism. *Warte Mal!*, like all Sidén's work, is based on content and on a personal and collective urgency in psychic dimensions, not on a pre-existing formal choice. The origin of the work is an inner necessity, not a concept of forms. The fact that the work only arrived by a roundabout route at a documentary form gives it a particular tension that sets it apart from most other documentary works.

In any interview, the interviewer is faced with a dilemma: whether to develop some special empathy and solidarity with the interviewee or whether to follow a prepared line. With the rapid spread of the interview as an artistic form in the late 1990s, visual artists learned this basic fact of journalism. Most documentary video works about the geo-political tensions in post-Communist Europe suffer from a certain *naïveté* in this matter. Ann-Sofi Sidén's work gives the impression that she is not touched by these potential traps and deficiencies in her chosen form. Her video works are never in danger of merely making a report or of taking up a stance for or against an issue, rather the documentary becomes an autonomous artistic form. This is due above all to the fact that Sidén is primarily interested in the direct visual representation of the psyche. The process and character of the pieces are mostly analogue to psychic processes at the border of normality. Her entire oeuvre, from the first performances to her feature films, her spatial installations and video works, revolves around the question of how the visual artist can most directly approach the psyche. This underlying artistic aim shapes her work down to the last detail, and also accounts for the fact that her interviews present universal images and life stories that go far beyond the actual topic of the work.

Warte Mal! is born out of a spontaneous 'choice' (in the sense of Sartre) focusing on women in an exemplary situation of exploitation: mass prostitution. *Warte Mal!,* therefore, underlines some feminist aspects of Sidén's work. After showing *Who Told The Chambermaid?* at *Manifesta 2*, Sidén received various invitations to participate in exhibition projects, including the one in Amsterdam that was to take place in the red-light district. The exhibition organizers offered the artist the chance to make direct contact with the prostitutes and the pimps. But because she felt constrained by the organization of the project, she diverted her attention to the Czech Republic. Various friends had previously told her about the mass prostitution at the eastern borders of Western Europe. The images had stuck so vividly in her imagination that she simply set off to see for herself. And the outcome was *Warte Mal!*: not commissioned by anyone, just driven by a deep, inner compulsion.

Translated from the German by Fiona Elliott

BIOGRAPHY

Born 1962 in Stockholm
Lives and works in Stockholm, Berlin and New York

Solo Exhibitions

2001   *Fidei Commissum*, Christine König Galerie, Vienna

Station 10 and Back Again, Norrköpings Konstmuseum

Ann-Sofi Sidén - The Panning Eye Revisited, Musée d'art Moderne de la Ville de Paris

2000   *2 DVD Installations: Eija-Liisa Ahtila & Ann-Sofi Sidén*, Contemporary Arts Museum, Houston

Who is invading my privacy, not so quietly and not so friendly?, South London Gallery, London

1999   *Warte Mal!*, Wiener Secession, Vienna

Galerie Barbara Thumm, Berlin

QM, I Think I Call Her QM, Bergen Fine Art Society, Bergen

Galerie Nordenhake, Stockholm

1995   *Excerpt III*, Gallery Lucas & Hoffman, Cologne

It is by confining one's neighbour that one is convinced of one's own sanity, Galerie Nordenhake, Stockholm

1993   *CODEX*, Riksutställningar

Group Exhibitions

2001   *Let's talk about Sex – Sexualitet und Körperlichkeit in der Gegenwart*, Kunst Haus Dresden

CTRL (Space), ZKM, Center for Art and Media, Karlsruhe

Trauma, Dundee Contemporary Arts; Firstsite, Colchester; MOMA, Oxford

Berlin Biennale für zeitgenössische Kunst, Kunst Werke, Berlin

2000   *Scène de la vie conjugale*, Villa Arson, Nice

Through Melancholia and Charm - Four Installations, Galerie Nordenhake, Berlin

Wanås 2000, Knislinge

Immodest Gazes, Fundació La Caixa, Barcelona

Kwangju Biennale 2000, Kwangju

Organising Freedom, Moderna Museet, Stockholm

1999   *Carnegie International 1999/2000*, Pittsburgh

Fireworks, De Appel, Amsterdam

Dial M for..., Kunstverein München

d'APERTutto, La Biennale di Venezia, (curated by Harald Szeemann)

Midnight Walkers & City Sleepers, Red Light District, Amsterdam

1998   *XXIV Bienal de São Paulo*

In Visible Light, Moderna Museet, Stockholm

Manifesta 2, Luxemburg

Arkipelag, Nordiska Museet, Stockholm

Nuit Blanche, Musée d'art Moderne de la Ville de Paris

1997	*Conspiracy*, Uppsala Konstmuseum, Uppsala
	Zonen der ver-störung, Steiricher Herbst, Graz (curated by Silvia Eiblmayr)
	Clean & Sane, Edsvik, Stockholm (curated by Maria Lind)
	Invasion, Saaremaa Biennial, Kingisepp
	Around Us, Inside Us, Borås Konstmuseum
	Letter & Event, Apex, New York
	1996 False Notions, Beam Gallery, Nijmegen, Netherlands
	Electronic Undercurrents, Statens Museum for Kunst, Copenhagen
1996	*See What it Feels Like*, Rooseum, Malmö
1995	*395'*, Sandvikens Konsthall
	Streets, Helsinki Art Hall, Helsinki
	A Tribute to Ingmar Bergman, Nordanstad Gallery, New York
	Strange Phenomena, National Museum, Helsinki
	Hybrid No. 4, The Kitchen, New York
1994	*Who Has Enlarged This Hole?*, Alice Fabian, 53 West 9th St., New York
	Good Morning America, PS.1 Studio Artist Group Show at PS.1 Museum, New York
	Revir, (Good Morning America), Kulturhuset, Stockholm
1993	*Brown Tableaux for Five Monitors*, Sundsvalls Museum
	Ad Hoc, Galerie Nordenhake, Stockholm
	Prospect, Fotografiska Museet, Stockholm
	Pimpinette: Ladies' Wear & Accessories, Villa Val Lemme
1992	*The City Stones*, video installation, Stockholm Stads Stadsmuseum
	Ecce Homo, Liljevalchs Konsthall, Stockholm
1991	*AVE, Audio Visual Art Festival*, Arnhem
	Swedish Avantgarde Film Program 1990-1994, (organized by Anthology Film Archives), New York

Performances and Happenings

1991	*Gretchens Monologue*, Fylkingen Stockholm (also as radiotheatre in collaboration with L. Ericsson)
1990	*Directaction, Queen of Mud Inspects the Art Fair*, Sollentuna
	179 Kg, Come and Go, Act-90, Kulturhuset, Stockholm
1989	*Queen of Mud Visits the Perfume Counter*, Varuhuset NK, Stockholm
1988	*TSSS, Greetings to the Swedish Farmers and their Asian Women*, Geneva

Film and video

2001	*Head Gallery Piss Up*, 11 min, video
2000	*Head Lake Piss Down*, 7 min. video
1999	*The Preparation*, video
1997	*Room IIII*, video by Ann-Sofi Sidén and Paul Giangrossi
	QM, I Think I Call Her QM, a film by Ann-Sofi Sidén and Tony Gerber, 28 min., 35mm colour film
1995	*The Trailer for Who is Queen of Mud?*, video
1994	*Every Six Weeks*, video

1993	*CODEX*, video
1991	*Sofi's Room*, video
1990	*Love Story*, video
1988	*Cookie Puss*, 16 mm
1987	*Life of a Sailor's Wife*, 16 mm
1986	*I Still Got My Memory*, video

Other activities

1999	Rotterdam Film festival
1998	First prize in Statens Konstråd's public sculpture contest Platser (Places), Stockholm
	Screening of *QM, I think I call her QM* at the Movie Theatre Zita, Stockholm
	Rum i Rum ('Room Within the Room') a surveillance installation for an electro-acoustic concert at SVR, the Radio House, Stockholm
1997	Theatre set design for *Henry IV*, by Pirandello, directed by Jonas Cornell at Stadtsteatern, Stockholm

Catalogues (solo exhibitions)

2001	*Ann-Sofi Sidén - The Panning Eye Revisited*, Musée d'art Moderne de la Ville de Paris, preface by Laurence Bossé, texts by Gertrud Sandqvist, Julia Garimorth, Alain Didier-Weill and Gregory Volk
2000	*Warte Mal!*, Wiener Secession, Vienna, with text by Erik van der Heeg
1998	*XXIV Bienal de São Paulo*, text by Maria Lind, interview by Mats Stjernstedt
1995	*No. 144. It is by confining one's neighbour, that one is convinced of one's own sanity*, UTICA Publishing. Excerpt from Alice Fabian's diary, text by Ann-Sofi Sidén
1993	*CODEX*, Published by Riksutställningar. Excerpt from court verdicts, 1500-1900 century, text by Maria Lind

Catalogues (group exhibitions)

2001	*Mirades Impúdiques*, Fundació la Caixa, Barcelona
2000	*Organising Freedom*, Moderna Museet, Stockholm
1999/2000	*Carnegie International*, Pittsburgh,
1999	*Composite/Sammensatt*, The National Museum of Contemporary Art, Oslo,
	Dial M for..., Kunstverein München. Text by Sabine Russ and Ann-Sofi Sidén
	La Biennale di Venezia 48, d'APERTutto. Text by Robert Fleck
1998	*In Visible Light*, Moderna Museet, Stockholm
	Manifesta 2, Luxemburg
	Nuits Blanches, Scènes nordiques: les années 90, Paris
1997	*Conspiracy*, Uppsala Konstmuseum. Text by Sabine Russ
	Zonen der Ver-störung, Steirscher Herbst, Graz, Austria. Text by Erik van der Heeg
	Clean & Sane, Edsvik, Stockholm. Text by Maria Lind
	Around Us, Inside Us, Borås Konstmuseum
	Invasion, Saaremaa Biennial, Estonia. Text by Erik van der Heeg
	Letter & Event, Apex Gallery, New York. Text by Maria Lind
1996	*See What it Feels Like*, Rooseum, Malmö. Text by Erik van der Heeg

1995   *Strange Phenomena*, National Museum, Helsinki. Text by Maria Lind,

1994   *Revir/Territory*, Kulturhuset, Stockholm. Text by Maria Lind

        P.S.1 Museum's studioprogram 1993/1994, New York

1993   *The Rules Of the Game*, Stockholm. Text: quotations from 18th century court verdicts of the City of Stockholm

1991   *Art Against AIDS*, Royal Academy, Stockholm. Swedish Avantgarde film 1924-1990, *Anthology Film Archive*, New York. Text by Ilmar Laaban

Articles/Texts

2001   Mats Stjernstedt, 'Ann-Sofi Sidén, Norrköpings Konstmuseumí, *Artforum*, September

        Geneviève Breerette, Gillian Wearing et Ann-Sofi Sidén, deux vidéastes en quête de réalité, *Le Monde*, 5 April

        Jan Estep, 'Feral Children and the Queen of Mud', *New Art Examiner*, March

        Lars O. Ericsson, 'Människor som du och jag', *Dagens Nyheter*, 15 March

2000   Gregory Volk, 'On Ann-Sofi Sidén's *Fidei Commissum*', *Camera Austria*, Nov.

        Harald Fricke, interview with Ann-Sofi Sidén, *Kunst-Bulletin*, Jan./Feb.

        Katy Siegel, '1999 Carnegie International', *Artforum*, January

1999   Roberta Smith, 'Carnegie International: Safe Among the Seamless Shadows', *The New York Times*, 17 Nov.

        Daniel Birnbaum, 'Shrink Rap', *Artforum*, Summer

        Maria Lind, 'Peeping on the Chambermaid', *Flash Art*, Summer

        Milou Allerholm, 'Ann-Sofi Sidén's installation is…', *NU: The Nordic Art Review*, January

1998   Daniel Birnbaum, 'All Together Now', *Frieze*, No. 42,

        Lars O. Ericsson, 'The Queen of Mud Strikes Again', *SIKSI*, No. 1, Justin Hoffman, 'Zonen der Ver-störung', *Kunstforum International*, No. 139, Dec. 1997-March 1998

1997   Daniel Birnbaum, 'Cumulus', *Parkett*, No. 50/51

        Sabine Russ, *Trans*,

        Daniel Birnbaum, 'Drömda landskap', *Dagens Nyheter*, 21 May

1996   Maria Lind, *Svenska Dagbladet*,

        Daniel Birnbaum *Artforum*, February

        Sarah Arrenius, 'A Mud Queen as TV-star', *Index*, No. 1,

1995   Erik van der Heeg, Daniel Birnbaum, 'The Diary Of a Lady who Disappeared', *Material*, No. 27,

        Ingela Lind, 'Som en Hitchcockfilm', *Dagens Nyheter*, 6 Sept.

        Milou Allerholm, 'Psykopatologens vardagsliv', *Expressen*, 11 Sept.

        Maria Lind, 'Med besatthet som råmaterial', *Svenska Dagbladet*, 9 Sept.

        Sara Arrhenius, 'Vem övervakar övervakarna?', *Aftonbladet*, 15 Sept.

1994   Kim Levin, 'Down the Rabbit Hole', *The Village Voice*, No. 27,

        David Lindsay, 'Mad House: Art That Imitates an Eccentric Life', *New York Post*

        Milou Allerholm, 'The Violence Of Everyday Life', *Index*, No. 3/4,

1993   Ingamaj Beck, 'Guds makt - och bödelns', *Aftonbladet*

        Ingamaj Beck, 'Metamorfoser', *Aftonbladet Kultur*

        Magnus Bärtås, '90-tal presenterar Maria Lindberg och Ann-Sofi Sidén', *90-tal*, No. 2/3

1991   Susanne Skoglund, *Bang*, No. 1

ARTIST'S ACKNOWLEDGEMENTS

This project was conceived with the support and encouragement of the following people and institutions to whom I would like to give my gratitude:

Foremost, Cederic Jabirek and Radek Cichon, my translators/ guides in the Czech Republic; Ivetta at 'La Strada' in Prague; Ludmilla at 'Karo' in Cheb for helping me organize three of the interviews; Lotta Ericsson for vital discussions and company on one of the trips; Hanna Göransson, Stockholm; Ivan and Camilla Miksovic, New York, who translated the interviews; Judy Elkan, New York, who transcribed subtitles and diary entries; IASPIS in Stockholm and Framtidens Kultur in Uppsala for generous funding; Hedwijg Feijn, who invited me to the 'Midnight Walker and City Sleeper' project in Amsterdam; Claes Nordenhake, Barbara Thumm and Sofia Bertilsson for being there; the Hayward Gallery, London, in particular Susan Ferleger Brades, Clare Carolin, Sophie Allen, Fiona Bradley and Linda Schofield for their sincere interest and engagement in this exhibition and book.

Thanks especially to Paul Giangrossi for editing and support. And my warmest thanks goes to all of the people frequenting the Motel Hubert, who have generously shared their daily lives with me and my translators during our several trips to Dubi.

All material was edited by myself with the assistance of the following people:
Paul Giangrossi, New York: The interviews with 'Eva' and 'Honza', the material used for the projections 'Dubi Morning'. 'Warte Mal!', 'Diary Entries' and 'The Green'.
Per Telijer, Stockholm: The interviews with 'The Police', 'Vanja', 'Kvéta'.
Jean at 'Mad Dog' in New York: The interviews with 'Katja', 'Petra', 'Klaus' and 'Miluse'.

All snap shots and video stills by myself, except a few that have been taken with my camera by the people involved.